The Way, The Truth & The Life Series

The Truth

Student's Book 8

Second Edition

By Sr Marcellina Cooney CP

Editorial Team

Doug Doherty, Angela Edwards, Angela Grady, Stephen Horsman,

James Jukes, Liz McCaul, Paul Moloney, Rachel Smith and Mary White

Publisher

Teachers' Enterprise in Religious Education Co. Ltd

Introduction

Welcome to this edition of 'The Truth' which complements 'The Way' and 'The Life'. In St. John's Gospel, Jesus calls each one of us individually and, together, as Church, to live in him, who is the 'Way, the Truth and the Life' (Jn. 14:6).

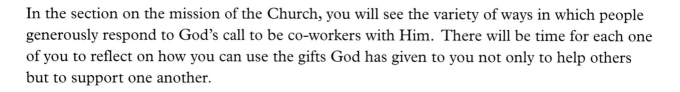

In 'The Truth', you will begin by studying Creation, not so much scientifically as theologically, that is, as the unfolding of God's plan for us and our world. You will have the opportunity to reflect on the Covenants God has made with Noah, Abraham and in greater depth the covenant with Moses. You will then prepare to celebrate the birth of Jesus and come to understand how he is the New Covenant.

Your study of theology becomes more challenging as you have the opportunity and privilege to explore the mystery of the Eucharist and the mystery of Jesus' passion, death and resurrection. You will be invited to think deeply and open your heart to understand events which took place over two thousand years ago and yet are made truly present in the Mass as celebrated throughout the whole world today.

In the section on the mission of the Church, you will see the variety of ways in which people generously respond to God's call to be co-workers with Him. There will be time for each one of you to reflect on how you can use the gifts God has given to you not only to help others but to support one another.

Finally, you will study aspects of the Church in Britain, starting with the arrival of the early Christians and focusing on some of the most momentous events which shaped the lives of many of our ancestors. By reflecting on the past, may we become ever more conscious of the opportunities we have to openly profess our faith in Jesus Christ!

My wish is that your studies this year will help you to grow closer to Jesus in faith, hope and love and that you will discover the promise his call holds for you.

✠ Vincent Nichols
Archbishop of Westminster

Contents

1. Creation

Know that God created and sustains the world.
Reflect on some of the wonders of Creation.

Praise of God

"The heavens proclaim the Glory of God
and the firmament shows forth the work of His hands.
Day unto day takes up the story
and night unto night makes known the message.

No speech, no word, no voice is heard
yet their span goes forth through all the earth,
their words to the utmost bounds of the world." (Ps. 18)

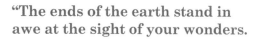

"The ends of the earth stand in awe at the sight of your wonders.

The lands of sunrise and sunset you fill with your glory."

"You care for the earth, give it water, you fill it with riches.

Your river in heaven brims over to provide its grain." (Ps. 64)

Activity

Meditate on the Power Point on 'The Seasons'.
What do these photos tell you about God?
Share with the person next to you.

Pause to Reflect

Listen to 'Close Your Eyes' (on DVD ROM).
Now watch the Power Point presentation on Winter,
Spring, Summer and Autumn.

Think of all the things these photos tell you about God.
Share with the person next to you.

The
Truth

The Way, The Truth
& The Life Series

God creates and sustains

The scriptures and the teaching of the Church tell us that:
*   God is responsible for everything in creation;
*   God created out of nothing;
*   nothing exists that does not owe its existence to God the Creator;
*   because God is infinitely good, creation reflects His goodness;
*   God created humankind in His own image and likeness;
*   God made humankind the stewards of creation.

We believe that everything that exists is totally dependent upon God's
power. That power of creation is
expressed in the Book of Genesis
in the words: 'Let there be light',
and there was light. In the same
way, if God were to say: 'Let
something stop being …' it would
cease to be. In other words, the
whole of creation and each one of
us depend wholly on God creating
and looking after us.

One of the most powerful psalms
in the Old Testament explains
how God is with us.

In Praise of God's Omniscience

"God, you examine me and know me,
you know when I sit, when I rise,
you understand my thoughts from afar.
You watch when I walk or lie down,
you know every detail of my conduct.

A word is not on my tongue
before you, O God, know all about it.
You fence me in, behind and in front,
you have laid your hand upon me.
Such amazing knowledge is beyond me,
a height to which I cannot attain.

If I speed away on the wings of the dawn,
if I dwell beyond the ocean,
even there your hand will be guiding me,
your right hand holding me fast.

You created my innermost self,
knit me together in my mother's womb.
For so many marvels I thank you;
A wonder am I, and all your works are
wonders."

(Extracts from Ps.139)

The world shares the power and energy of God. God's continuous creative activity is a little bit like the continual flow of digital signals which provide a picture on our TV screen. If God were to withdraw His creative energy or power, then everything would collapse back into nothing again. So God accompanies His creation and remains close to all His creatures. It is important to remember that God is still working, still creating, redeeming and sanctifying us. The wonder and awe of His creation inspired not only the Psalmist but also poets, musicians and artists. Elizabeth Barrett Browning wrote:

**"Earth's crammed with Heaven
And every common bush afire with God,
But only he who sees takes off his shoes,
The rest sit round it and pluck blackberries!"**

Activities

1. Listen to the recording of Psalm 139 (DVD ROM) or use your Bible to read it.
   Choose three lines that mean most to you.
   Write them into your book and say why you chose them.

2. "God does not create to forget but creates and sustains." Discuss.
   a) Say what you **think** and **why**.
   b) Give a different point of view and say why some people hold it.
   c) Say why you **disagree** with it.
   d) Quote some source of evidence.

3. a) Research the work of an artist, poet, musician of your choice who celebrates the glory of creation, for example, Gerard Manley Hopkins SJ, John Keats, William Wordsworth, Benjamin Britten, Gustav Holst, Felix Mendelsohn, Vincent van Gogh, William Turner, Christy Nolan, Ted Hughes, Seamus Heaney.
   b) Present your research to the class using audio and/or visual support.

Understand the theological truths in the accounts of Creation in Genesis. Reflect on their importance for us.

Interpreting the Bible

The Church teaches that the Holy Spirit enlightened and assisted the biblical writers in a divine way. However, the Spirit left the writers free to use their own talents and resources in the process. Because of this we can say that the Bible is the Word of God in the words of the authors.

The Bible is inspired. This means that it is free from error in matters that relate to our salvation. It does not mean that the Spirit protected the biblical writers from historical and scientific error. God never intended them to compose books on science and history.

The Bible contains theological truths, that is, truths about our relationship with God and with one another. They are about us in this world. Scientific truths are also about this world but they are based on facts that can be proven scientifically.

The Creation Story in Genesis

The people of the Old Testament wanted to know about the creation of the universe. In order to help their readers to understand the mysterious action of God, the writers of Genesis used symbolic stories to get across important **theological truths**.

Vatican Observatory

For thousands of years, academics have argued over these creation stories.
Let us listen to a discussion.

 DVD: 'The Creation' Radio discussion

Beliefs about Creation

The following are examples of some of the beliefs held by different groups.

Dr. Know-it says:
The story of Creation is a fairy tale for children. We're grown up now. We know that the big bang started the world. We know it was sheer chance over billions of years that led to a planet like ours. Life developed and became more complex over billions of years. This was evolution. The story of the six-day-Creation is like the story of Santa Claus: a myth to outgrow.

Mr. Read-it says:
The Book of Genesis states quite clearly that God created the universe in six days and on the seventh day he sat back and admired it. There is no way in which God can lie, so all that is written in Genesis is absolutely true. We all know that the human race started with Adam and Eve who had lots of children and so the population grew.

Miss Believe-it says:
I go along with both of you, but not totally. Let me explain. The truths contained in the Book of Genesis are 'theological truths' – not 'scientific truths'. They help explain our relationship with God, with our environment and with each other. We might not believe these days that the world was actually created in six days, but we do believe God created it over a period of time and that he loves us.

Activities

1. Choose a tree, plant, flower or leaf. Describe in
   a) a scientific way;
   b) a theological way how it came into existence.

2. Explain:
   a) how people who believe in God understand the story of creation;
   b) how some scientists understand the story.

3. Think about this statement:
   "It is not possible to be a scientist and believe in God".
   a) Say what you **think** and **why**.
   b) Give a different point of view and say why some people hold it.
   c) Say why you **disagree** with it.
   d) Quote some source of evidence from people who have expressed views on this subject.

**Know that we are made in the image and likeness of God.
Reflect on what this means for us.**

Made in God's Own Image

"God said, '**Let us make man in our own image, in the likeness of ourselves, and let them be masters of the fish of the sea, the birds of heaven, the cattle, all the wild beasts and all the reptiles that crawl upon the earth'.**

**God created man in the image of Himself,
In the image of God He created him,
Male and female He created them.**

God blessed them, saying to them, 'Be fruitful, multiply, fill the earth and subdue it'." (Gen. 1:26-28)

This is You

You are made in God's own image.
You are free to use the powers God has given to you:
> the courage to love
> the power to think
> the freedom to choose
> the ability to decide for yourself
> the mastery of the world itself,
> and the right to make good use of all that God has created.

You show God to others when you are really YOU,
when you reflect God in your own way.
> This is what it means to be a person.
> This is what it means to be you.
> How often do you think of thanking God
> for making you to be **you?**

Activity

a) Reflect on the poem 'This is you'.
b) Illustrate the powers God has given to you with simple images.
c) Give examples to show how you use these powers in your life.
d) Think of one thing you could do in order to be more like God.

The Dignity of the Human Person

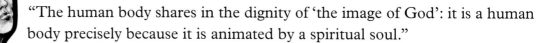

"The human body shares in the dignity of 'the image of God': it is a human body precisely because it is animated by a spiritual soul."

"The unity of the soul and body is so profound that one has to consider the soul to be the 'form' of the body. That means, it is because of its spiritual soul that the body made of matter becomes a living, human body. However, it is not two natures united, but rather their union forms a single nature."

"The Church teaches that every spiritual soul is created immediately by God. It is, therefore, not 'produced' by the parents. It is also immortal. That means it does not perish when it separates from the body at death; it will be reunited with the body at the final Resurrection."

(Catechism of the Catholic Church paragraphs 364-366).

Pause to Reflect

- Your body is given a spiritual life because you have a soul.
- Your soul is created by God; it is not given to you by your parents.
- Your soul and body form one human nature.
- When your body dies, your soul will live on in eternity and be united with your body in the final Resurrection.

Can you Explain

1. What are the two main differences between the body and the soul?
2. What are the needs of the body?
3. What are the needs of the soul?
4. Can the body exist without the soul?
5. Can the soul exist without the body?
6. What do you need to nourish your spiritual life?

Our Human Ecology

There is a growing concern in the world about the ecology of the earth. But little is mentioned about human ecology, that is, about our interior life, the way we understand and nurture our innermost selves. Each one of us is a spiritual being. That's the truth. And it is only God's Spirit that can fulfil and satisfy our deepest nature. Take time to be alone with God, He is the source of all true inner peace and happiness. 'No God, no peace. Know God, know peace'.

St. Augustine tells us that our hearts are restless until they rest in God. He assures us that "God loves each one of us as if there were only one of us to love". God invites us into a living, vibrant, demanding relationship with Him. This life of faith in God is an adventure, not for the faint hearted, but for those with courage, prepared to risk living a life that matters.

A Life that Matters

"Anything you do from the soul-full self will help lighten the burdens of the world. Anything!

You have no idea what the smallest word; the tiniest generosity can cause to be set in motion.

Be outrageous in forgiving.
Be dramatic in reconciling.

Mistakes? Back up and make them as right as you can, then move on.
Be off the charts in kindness.

In whatever you are called to, strive to be devoted to it in all aspects large and small.
Fall short? Try again.
Mastery is made in increments, not in leaps.

Be brave, be fierce, be visionary!
Mend the parts of the world that are within your reach.

To strive to live this way is the most dramatic gift you can ever give to the world."

Clarissa Pinkola Estés

 **Activities**

1. In pairs: study the reflection, 'A Life that Matters'.
   a) What is your first impression of it?
   b) Write down the five phrases or words that you find most helpful.
   c) Explain why you find these helpful.

2. "We are God's work of art, created in Christ Jesus to live the good life as from the beginning he had meant us to live it." (Eph. 2:10). How might this belief inspire and influence you and others? Discuss.
   Think about:
   - *treatment of our bodies*
   - *relationships with others.*

De-creation!

The presence of evil in our world raises many questions. If God created everything good, how did evil enter the world? In the Book of Genesis the biblical writers tell what happened in a symbolic story.

It begins with the snake entering the garden of paradise and speaking to the woman:

"'Did God really tell you not to eat from any tree in the garden?'

'We may eat the fruit of any tree in the garden except the tree in the middle of it', the woman answered. 'God told us not to eat the fruit of that tree or even to touch it; if we do, we will die.'

The snake replied, 'That's not true; you will not die. God said that because he knows that when you eat it you will be like God and know what is good and what is bad'."

Read Genesis 3:6-20.

Pause to Reflect

We have only to watch the news on television to hear about violence and all kinds of tragic events in our world.

No one seems to escape from suffering in one form or another. *Where, why, how* are some of the questions we ask?

What are the current events which cause us to ask these questions?

In groups: prepare a 'Prayer Service for People in Need'.

- Choose one part of the world in need of prayer.
- Find appropriate symbols, prayers, music or song.
- Share your plan with the rest of the class.
- Find a special time to put on your 'Prayer Service'.
- Invite others in the schools to pray with you.

Key Theological Truths in Genesis:

- God created man and woman out of love.
- He created them in a state of holiness, which means, in a relationship of friendship with Him.
- God created them in His own image and likeness.
- He gave them the gift of 'freedom', so that they could freely be His friends.
- From the very beginning man and woman were given the freedom to choose between good and evil.
- God told them to increase and multiply so they became the 'first parents' of all human beings.

- However, our 'first parents' Adam and Eve were tempted by the Evil One.
- They misused their God-given gift of 'freedom' to turn against their Creator.
- They chose to find their own self-fulfilment apart from God.
- By turning against God they lost their friendship and happiness with Him.
- God had intended His original plan of friendship with Him for all human beings so, because of the disobedience of Adam and Eve, this sin has been passed on to all of us.

Original Sin

As members of the human race our human nature is wounded by the 'first sin' and our freedom is weakened.

What does it mean for us?

"When tempted by the devil, the first man and woman allowed trust in their Creator to die in their hearts. In their disobedience they wished to become 'like God' but without God and not in accordance with God (Gen: 3:5). Thus Adam and Eve immediately lost for themselves and for all their descendants the original grace of holiness and justice."
(Compendium Catechism of the Catholic Church 75)

What is Original Sin?

The first sin known as "original sin, in which all human beings are born, is the state of deprivation of original holiness and justice... it remains a mystery which we cannot fully understand". (Compendium Catechism of the Catholic Church 76)

How does the account of Original Sin help us?

It tells us that our human nature has been 'wounded' by original sin. While original sin is removed when we receive the Sacrament of Baptism, we still suffer from the effects of that sin, that is, we are left with a tendency towards sin.

Here are some examples.
* We experience feelings of envy, the desire to dominate others or to 'get even' when things go wrong.

* We have a tendency to be selfish, that is, just to think of what we want for ourselves and not to consider the needs of others.

* In a subtle way, when we have not faced the truth we can convince ourselves that we have acted justly.

* We recognise great injustice in the world but have difficulty finding a remedy.

We know now that these evil tendencies are not from God; they are the result of the first act of disobedience and selfishness by our first parents. Fortunately, the Bible goes on to explain how God works in wonderful ways to restore our friendship with Him.

Activities

1. Think of times when making a wrong choice has spoilt things for you and others at school or at home.
   a) Describe what happened.
   b) What effect did it have on you and others?
   c) What would you do if you were in that same situation today?
   d) What beliefs and values may inspire you to act differently?

2. "The more one does what is good, the freer one becomes. There is no true freedom except in the service of what is good and just. The choice to disobey and do evil is an abuse of freedom and leads to 'slavery of sin'." (Catechism of the Catholic Church 1733)
   Explain what this statement means and give examples to demonstrate it.

3. "The most Blessed Virgin Mary was, from the first moment of her conception, by a singular grace and privilege of almighty God and by virtue of the merits of Jesus Christ, Saviour of the human race, preserved immune from all stain of original sin." (CCC 491)

   a) Explain in your own words what the Church teaches about the Virgin Mary's Immaculate Conception.
   b) Where else can you find evidence that Mary was without sin?
      (Clues: St. Luke's Gospel; a traditional prayer of the Church and a place of pilgrimage)
   c) Explain how belief in the Immaculate Conception has inspired and influenced people for many generations.

**Understand God's call to stewardship.
Reflect on our response to it.**

God's call to Stewardship

God is the Creator of everything there is and creation reflects God's goodness. It glorifies and worships God in continuous praise. Nature reveals God to us and allows us to experience God's presence.

When God created people, He said:
'Let [them] have dominion over the fish in the sea and over the birds of the air, and over the cattle, and over all the wild animals of the earth, and over every creeping thing that creeps upon the earth' (Gen. 1:26).

We have received the special gift and challenge of sharing in God's creative activity.
As 'co-creators', then, our acts should reflect God's own love for creation. So our care for creation can be a true expression of our praise and thanksgiving to God.

Pause to Reflect

Tune in to your conscience!
- List all the things you do to care for the environment.
- Think of what more you could do and write it down.
- What worries you most about the state of the environment?

The Stewards' Response

The way we live and the choices we make affect the lives of others, not only human life but all forms of life on earth. Damage to the environment affects every part of creation. It affects the poor most of all.

God has more than generously provided for human beings in the lavish natural resources of the universe.

It is our misuse and abuse of the natural resources that are putting an enormous strain on the environment.

Activity

"It's man's greed not man's need that has created the imbalance in the universe." Discuss the religious and moral implications of this in the light of Matthew 25:40.

- Say what you **think** and **why**.
- Give a different point of view and say why some people hold it.
- Say why you **disagree** with it.
- Quote some source of evidence.

Creation reveals human sin

"Our capacity to marvel at the earth, but also to develop and utilise its resources (for instance through the application of science and technology), has greatly enriched our lives. This human creativity carries with it a profound responsibility. However, it is also part of Christian faith to recognise that we are sinners. This truth means that sin has distorted the human relationship with the natural world: we have disturbed the balance of nature in radical and violent ways." (The Call of Creation, Bishops' Conference of England & Wales).

Forests are often described as the lungs of the earth. In some parts of the world they are reduced to wasteland.

Emissions of 'greenhouse gases' continue to affect the atmosphere in ways that threaten the balance of life on the planet. As a result, climate change is severely disrupting the lives of humankind.

Eighty per cent of the world's resources are with the richest twenty per cent of the population.

On an average, twenty per cent of the population remain destitute. They lack even the basic necessities of clean water, adequate food, shelter and clothing.

Blessed Mother Teresa reminds us that: "Suffering today is because people are hoarding, not giving, not sharing. Jesus made it very clear. Whatever you do to the least of my brethren, you do it to me. Give a glass of water, you give it to me. Receive a little child, you receive me".

Activities

1. Read about 'Ryan's Well (Teacher's Book) and look at the Power Point on the DVD.
   a) Go to www.ryanswell.ca. Find out about the 'Ripple Effect'.
   b) What reply do you think Ryan would give to people who say, 'Why should I bother?' or 'What difference will it make?'

2. On Ryan's website find 'Faith Based Initiatives'.
   a) Each person in the class should choose a different 'initiative' to study.
   b) In groups, share the 'initiative' you studied and select the most impressive one to relate to the whole class.
   c) As a class, decide on an 'initiative' to take and when you have done it send details of it to Ryan to put on his website.

3. Work in pairs or groups:
   Plan an Assembly.
   You must include:
   a) a brief description of an environmental issue, e.g. endangered species, wasting food, pollution, global warming;
   b) an explanation of why this issue is an abuse of God's Creation;
   c) a statement of Christian teaching on stewardship;
   d) suggestions for action that pupils can take in order to be responsible stewards in the school and neighbourhood;
   e) a prayer or choose a hymn to conclude the Assembly.

Be alive to the Glory of God

Throughout history, there have been people who remind us that the earth is God's gift to us and that we should take care of it and work with it to sustain life on this planet.

St. Francis of Assisi (1181-1226)

In 1979, Pope John Paul II made St. Francis Patron Saint of Ecology. He is well known for his love of animals, the taming of a fierce wolf and how he talked to the birds, but did you know that St Francis would lift a worm from the path in case it might be crushed? He asked for wild flowers to be left in the garden so that they could flourish and glorify their Creator.

Francis came to view all created things: animals, flowers, birds, insects, water, trees, fish, rocks, even the climate as his brothers and sisters because they are created and loved by God, our Father.

In a Franciscan view of the world, every element in the universe is related and interdependent: humans, animals, flowers, birds, insects, water, trees, fish, rocks, even the climate. As brothers and sisters to each other, we have a responsibility to care for one another.

 Activity

Read the 'Canticle of Brother Sun by St. Francis of Assisi'. (TB and DVD ROM)
Imagine you are St. Francis. Prepare a 60 Second Sermon for the people and the birds who flock to hear you preach!
Use words which will:
- awaken people to the beauty of creation;
- encourage them to lavish care on and protect the environment;
- inspire them to give thanks to God.

Blessed Kateri Tekakwitha, Model Ecologist (1656-1680)

Kateri's parents were native America Indians from different tribes. Her mother was a Catholic Algonquin and her father a Mohawk chief. Her parents and baby brother died from smallpox when Kateri was only four years old. She survived the smallpox but was left with a badly scarred face and almost blind. Kateri was adopted by her aunt and uncle.

When the Jesuit priests came to the village and opened a church, Kateri asked to be instructed in the faith. Her uncle and the rest of the family and tribe viewed the 'Black Robes' and their strange religion with suspicion and were angry at Kateri's determination to become a Catholic. Despite this, Kateri continued to learn more about Jesus and when she was twenty she was baptised.

She was threatened with torture, so she escaped from the family and tribe and travelled two hundred miles in very difficult conditions across woods, swamps and rivers to reach the Catholic Mission of St. Francis Xavier at Sault Saint Louis near Montreal. Her faith sustained her and on Christmas Day 1677, she made her First Holy Communion.

Kateri was unable to read and write but people gathered round her to hear her re-tell stories from the Bible. She helped those in the village who were poor or sick. She used to make crosses out of sticks and place them throughout the woods. These crosses reminded her to spend a few moments in prayer. She made her own little chapel in the woods by marking a tree with a cross and spent time in prayer there, even kneeling in the snow.

Kateri became ill and weak but in spite of all the advice to take care of herself, she continued to work for others. She died at the early age of twenty-four. Shortly after her death, her face, which had been scarred and disfigured, cleared and became beautiful.

Kateri is known as the 'Lily of the Mohawks". She was beatified in 1980 by Pope John Paul II and in 2002 he named her as patroness for World Youth Day.

Activities

1. Kateri has been called 'Lily of the Mohawks'; 'Model Ecologist' and in 2002 'Patroness of World Youth Day'. Why do you think she has been given these titles?

2. Kateri found God in peace and quiet in the woods, in the chapel before the Blessed Sacrament and in people. Where do different people find God today?

3. What small symbols do you have which remind you to pray?

Sister Dorothy Stang (1931–2005)

It was Saturday, 12th February 2005. Sister Dorothy had just returned from the small village in the Amazon. She had gone to take clothes and food to families whose homes had been burned down by logging companies. The logging companies were determined to drive out the poor farmers. She was on her way to meet more farmers to see what could be done about this worsening situation when two gunmen shot her six times at point blank range. She died on the muddy road.

When Sister Dorothy went to the Amazon in 1966, her mission was to help poor people, especially women and children in the most abandoned places. She wanted the farmers and their families to be able to live in peace.

Sister Dorothy lived in a very small house deep in the woods with no running water or electricity and was very happy there. She helped train agricultural workers, created a fruit factory, taught people to read and write, opened schools for the children and helped to train teachers.

While Sister Dorothy was recognised globally for her work in defending the human rights of the poor, she became a target for those who wanted her work stopped. She had a burning desire to help the poor even though this led her into some very dangerous political situations. She was ready to give her life to help them. She saw how they were being harassed, their houses and crops burned and some of the people murdered. She was not concerned about her own safety, only the safety of 'her people'. She studied their documents about land reform so that she could teach them about their legal rights.

It was her life of prayer and meditation on the Bible that gave her the vision, the strength and the courage to live for others.

Activities

1. Watch the Power Point presentation on Sister Dorothy Stang.
   Explain what you think were the religious beliefs and teachings that influenced her work.

2. Imagine you were Sister Dorothy's close friend. To what extent would you have warned, encouraged or supported her.
   Give reasons.

3. Find out what is now happening to the rain forests in the Amazon.
   a) What impact is it having on the environment?
   b) What is happening to the lives of the poor farmers now?
   c) Is there anything we can do to help? Make suggestions.

4. Think about your local area. What can be done to help the residents:
   • respect it;
   • improve it;
   • appreciate it;
   • understand that it is God's creation and we are the stewards.

5. Choose an area of natural environment that you know.
   a) Make a list of:
      • three things that you feel contribute to protecting it;
      • three things that might be damaging it.
   b) Explain what you could do to help protect and enrich the good things.
   c) What could be done to lessen the damaging elements?
   d) From a religious point of view why should you be concerned about the environment? Give three reasons.

2. The Covenant

What is a Covenant?

Let us suppose you have one hundred pounds and you decide to share equally with nine friends. What share is left for you?

Imagine you have total **power**, then, you decide to share it with nine others. How much will you have left? One tenth of what you had when you began.

Now let us suppose that you decide to share, not money or power, but **love**, or **friendship**, or **trust** with nine others. How much do you have left? Will your share be greater or smaller than when you started?

Your share will be greater; perhaps even nine times greater! Why? It is because **love**, **friendship** and **trust** are things that only exist when they are shared. We can call them 'covenantal goods'. The more we share these, the more we have.

In contrast, money and power are zero-sum games. If I win, you lose. If you win, I lose. Covenantal goods are non-zero-sum games, meaning, if I win, you also win. This has huge consequences for us.

Where do we find covenantal goods like love, friendship and trust? They are born, not in business companies, but in marriages, families and some communities.

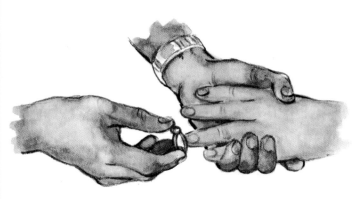

Think of the difference between *contracts* and *covenants*. In business, contracts are signed and each person does this to protect their own interests. A covenant is something different. In a covenant, two or more individuals come together in a deep bond of love and trust, to share their interests, sometimes even their lives, by pledging their faithfulness to one another. In this way, they do together what neither can achieve alone. (Adapted from address by Chief Rabbi Jonathan Sacks to the Lambeth Conference, July '08)

To summarize, **a covenant is a very deep and solemn bond of love and trust.** God will never break His covenant with us. We will see this in the life of Noah, Abraham, Moses, David and then in the new covenant Jesus makes with us. This covenant is what allows us to face the future without fear because we know we are not alone.

 **Activities**

1. Create a drama which illustrates the difference between a contract and sharing covenantal goods.

2. a) Would a visitor to your school find that relationships were based on a covenant or a contract? Why?
   b) Which would be better? How might it work out?

God's Covenant with Noah

The first covenant in the Bible is the one God made with Noah and through him with all of us. It is the story of a great flood that covered the earth because the people had become very selfish and corrupt. Only Noah was found to be just and upright – and so he survived with his family. They sailed across the flood in a large boat or ark, with animals of every kind on board.

When the flood receded, God sent the rainbow as a sign that He would never destroy His creation again. God made this covenant not only with Noah and all human beings but with all life on earth.

That promise is still true today; God is always faithful to a promise. However, we need to remember that God could not promise that *we* will never destroy the world because He has given us free will.

 Activity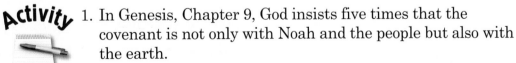

1. In Genesis, Chapter 9, God insists five times that the covenant is not only with Noah and the people but also with the earth.
   a) Read the chapter.
   b) Write out three references to all forms of life on the earth.

2. There are many natural disasters around the world. In groups, discuss
   a) the causes of such disasters;
   b) what we could do to lessen their destructive impact.
   Present your conclusions to the rest of the class in an interesting way.

God's Covenant with Abraham

When Abraham was very, very old God made a covenant with him.

"I will make a covenant with you," God told Abraham.

"This is what you must do. I am God. You must believe in Me and only worship Me. You must walk in My ways and live as I ask."

"This is what I shall do. I shall keep this covenant I have made with you. I shall give you many descendants and you will be the father of many nations... The covenant I have made with you will last forever... I shall call you by the name of Abraham, and your wife will be called Sarah from now on. I shall bless her and give her a son..."

"Sarah will have a baby and she will call him Isaac. Then I shall keep the covenant I have made with Isaac, just as I said."

Abraham fell on his face and laughed. The thought of his wife having a baby, when she was well past child bearing age, was just too much (Gen. 17:1-9, 15-19, 21). However, God was faithful to His covenant and Sarah gave birth to Isaac.

God has promised that he would look after His Chosen People. They were known as the Hebrews after the language they spoke and Israelites, the name they gave to the land where they settled. Later, they became known as Jews.

The covenant with Abraham is passed on, father to son, through each of these generations.

Activity

1. a) Watch the Power Point presentation on Abraham.
    b) Use bullet points to show what God asked Abraham to do. Start with the first time God spoke to him and what God promised him in return.
    c) How might Abraham's experience help you and other people in a variety of situations?

Here are some of Abraham's descendants:

Isaac married Rebekah. (1)

Esau and Jacob were Isaac and Rebekah's children. (2)

God appeared to Jacob and gave him the new name of Israel. (3)

Israel had twelve sons, his favourite was Joseph. This made the others angry. (4)

The brothers sold Joseph as a slave into Egypt. (5)

Eventually, Joseph was given an important position in Pharaoh's court. (6)

During a great famine the brothers came to Egypt to buy food. (7)

God worked through Joseph to provide for his brothers in Egypt. (8)

Activities

1. "Contracts benefit but covenants transform." Explain what this means. Give examples of the process of transformation that took place in Abraham's life through his covenant with God. Think about:
   - God's call and Abraham's response;
   - God's promise of a son;
   - God's request for sacrifice.

2. When things go wrong we are sometimes tempted to ask, 'Where is God?'
   Watch the Power Point presentation on Joseph.
   Identify at least four ways in which God was with Joseph.

Know that God chose Moses to lead His people towards the Promised Land.
Reflect on God's choice of leader.

The Covenant Unfolds

The Israelites settled in Egypt during the time of the famine. At first, they were well treated, but after the death of Joseph the Egyptians began to worry about the growing number of Israelites. As a result, a new Pharaoh gave instructions that all their baby boys were to be killed. In order to protect her son, an Israelite woman hid him in a reed basket on the river Nile. He was found and rescued by the Pharaoh's daughter; she gave him the name Moses. He was brought up in the palace as a royal prince.

Pause to Reflect

Watch the Power Point of the story of Moses. (DVD ROM)

The
Truth

THE WAY, THE TRUTH
& THE LIFE SERIES

Meanwhile, the Israelites became slaves of the Egyptians and were forced to do very hard work. When Moses grew up he came across an Egyptian striking an Israelite slave, one of his own countrymen, and, in a moment of fury, he killed the Egyptian and hid him in the sand. Others knew of his crime and Moses was forced to flee to Midian. There he settled, married and became a shepherd.

Back in Egypt, the Israelites were being very badly treated. The Egyptians were superior to them in every way: they had powerful armies, great temples, enormous wealth and a fertile country. The Israelites were powerless slaves with no country of their own but they wanted to be free. They remembered that God promised that He would look after them. He had made a covenant with them and God always keeps His word. So when the people prayed to God in their misery and slavery, He answered their prayers (Ex. 2:23-25).

God calls Moses

One day, Moses was looking after the flock of his father-in-law when an incredible thing happened: he saw a bush that was blazing but it was not being burnt up. God called to him from the middle of the bush.

"Moses, Moses!" **"Here I am,"** he answered. God said:

"I have seen the miserable state of my people…. I send you to Pharaoh to bring the sons of Israel, my people, out of Egypt" (Ex. 3:10).

However, Moses felt he would not be able to undertake such a difficult task and said to God: **"Who am I to go to Pharaoh and bring the sons of Israel out of Egypt?"** God said: **"I shall be with you"** (Ex. 3:12).

"What if they will not believe me and listen to my words…?" (Ex.4:1).

"But, my Lord, never in my life have I been a man of eloquence, either before or since you have spoken to your servant. I am a slow speaker and not able to speak well." (Ex. 4:10-11)

God said: **"Now go, I shall help you to speak and tell you what to say"**. God told Moses to take his brother Aaron to help him speak to the Pharaoh, King of Egypt.

Pause to Reflect

The only reassurance that Moses had from God was: **"I will be with you"**. It means:
  • Do not be afraid!
  • It's not you who is asked to do the work, I ask you only to let me do through you, what I wish to do.
  • I will be with you through it all.
  • Just trust in me, have confidence in me.
  • I want your cooperation and help, but let me decide the work you have to do. You think about how to do it.

Think deeply. How would you have responded?

Activities

1. Moses had difficulty believing he was the right man for the job God was asking him to do.
   a) What did God ask Moses to do?
   b) Give three reasons why he didn't want to do it.

2. Imagine you are Moses. You go home and tell Zipporah, your wife, what has happened. Talk over with her:
   • your fears;
   • what God has asked you to do;
   • the qualities you will need;
   • the possible dangers and difficulties.
   Write a summary of your conversation and your wife's response.

3. How could you use this story of Moses to help someone facing a difficult challenge today?

Moses returned to Egypt

Moses returned to Egypt to tell the Israelites that God had heard their prayers and was going to lead them out of Egypt and away from their miserable lives of slavery.

However, when Moses and his brother Aaron went to see the Pharaoh, the king of the Egyptians, they were not welcomed at all.

Use your Bible...
What are the key issues in the first audience that Moses had with the Pharaoh? (Ex.5:1-9).

The Plagues

God, through Moses, commanded the Pharaoh nine times: "Let my people go…" Each time Pharaoh refused. So God sent nine plagues that caused widespread destruction throughout Egypt. Eventually, the Pharoah was given one last chance. Unless the Israelites were allowed to leave, Moses told him, the eldest sons of all the Egyptians, including the Pharaoh's own, would die.

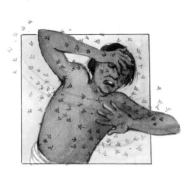   

Activities

Use your Bible to read about the plagues.
(Exodus, chapters 7-11).
  a) Write a short description of each one and
     give the reference.
  b) Why did the plagues go from bad to worse?
  c) Who was to blame and who suffered most?
  d) What is the important message for leaders of
     all countries today?

Use the Power Point presentation on DVD ROM to check your work.

HOLY BIBLE

The Passover

The Israelites were given instructions to make sure that it was obvious which houses belonged to them: no harm would come to people inside. They were also told to get ready for the journey. These were the preparations they had to make.

They had to cook and eat a special meal. It was to be roast lamb, served with bitter herbs and with bread made without yeast, because they wouldn't have time to wait for the bread to rise. This was known as unleavened bread. Any bit of the roast lamb that wasn't eaten had to be burnt.

They had to be ready for a quick getaway after the meal. With shoes and coats on, they had to eat standing up, so that they would be able to leave immediately, as soon as the Pharaoh gave the word.

They were to mark the doorframes of their houses with blood from the lamb prepared for the meal. That would be a clear sign that these were the homes of Israelites, not Egyptians.

God is Faithful

The Lord was true to His word. That night, after the eldest son of every Egyptian family had died, the Pharaoh agreed to let the Israelites go. Their own sons had been spared: the angel of death had passed over their houses. That is why they called this event the Passover, and why the Jews still celebrate the Passover to this very day.

Slavery Today

The workers' stories

There are two million garment workers in Bangladesh, and eighty-five percent of them are young women, between sixteen and twenty-five years old. Each year they sew £1.5 billion worth of clothing for export to Europe, and another £1.08 billion for the USA. Here are their stories.

Long hours and late pay

Women sewing garments for one of the best-known entertainment companies in the world are forced to work from 8.00 a.m. - 10.00 p.m., fourteen hours a day, seven days a week, for just ten pence an hour. They are allowed one day off in four months. They are cheated of their overtime and paid late.

Recently, when a group of workers asked if their wages could be paid on time, the manager slapped one of them, screaming, 'How dare you come into my office?' After the manager made a call on his mobile phone, five gang members carrying pistols arrived, and they punched and kicked twenty of the workers. Later the police arrived and arrested and imprisoned eight of the workers for two weeks.

The workers faced prison sentences on trumped-up charges. Of course they were fired. Their back wages were stolen. They may have to go into hiding.

Dame Anita Roddick, Founder, the Body Shop

Activities

1. Slavery today: "If shirts could only speak, if we would only listen".
   a) Read the account above of Anita Roddick's experience of slavery in Bangladesh.
   b) Work in groups. Think about what you could do to highlight or remedy the injustice that is taking place either in Bangladesh or elsewhere.
   c) Draw up an action plan.

2. Why do you think some people would choose to have a slave or slaves? Give reasons to explain why slavery is wrong.

The Passover Today

For over 3,000 years, Jews, who are descended from the ancient Israelites, have celebrated Passover to this very day. For them, it not only recalls their escape from Egypt and slavery, but also the start of their own nation. Most importantly, it is a celebration of God's goodness and faithfulness to the **Covenant**.

God commanded the Israelites to mark their freedom with an annual festival called **Pesach**. For the Jews, it commemorates their total reliance on God's help, for no human power could have taken them out of slavery. The Pesach lasts for eight days but the first night is the most important one. The celebration takes the form of a special meal called the **Seder**. Everyone makes a big effort to be with their family, even if they live away from home. It is the most important family event of the year. Cushions are put on everyone's chair so that they can be comfortable. It is a sign of freedom which slaves are not permitted.

The meal follows a special order that is set down in a book known as the **Hagadah** (telling of the story).

At every Seder (Passover Meal), the youngest member of the family asks the head of the household questions.

Why is this night different from all other nights?
- *On all other nights we may eat chametz or matzah. Tonight, why do we eat only matzah?*
- *On all other nights we may eat any kind of herbs. Tonight, why do we eat bitter herbs?*

During the Seder these questions are answered as the family read through the Hagadah. For example, the head of the household takes half of the middle matzah out of the dish and says:

"Blessed art thou, O Lord, our God, King of the universe, who hast sanctified us with thy commandments, and commanded us to eat unleavened cakes".

"Blessed art thou, O Lord, our God, King of the universe, who hast sanctified us with thy commandments, and commanded us to eat bitter herbs".

The story is not only told through words; each item of food on the Seder plate is a symbol calling to mind a different aspect of the story. Because the Jews are celebrating the passage from slavery to freedom most of the symbolic foods have associations with both slavery and freedom.

The bone is a symbol of the Passover sacrifice. It is a reminder of how God passed over the houses of the Israelites while smiting the Egyptians. The bitter herbs are a reminder of how bitter the lives of the Israelites were in Egypt. The matzah (bread made without yeast) is a reminder of how the Israelites left Egypt in such a hurry that they were unable to allow their dough to rise. Each person is given a glass of wine. An extra glass is filled with wine for the prophet Elijah and the door is opened for a while to encourage his arrival. This arrival would signify the coming of the Messianic Age and the end of all oppression.

The Seder plate goes in the middle of the table with the following items on it:

Roasted egg
It symbolises the burnt offering once made to God in the Temple.

Roasted bone
It is a reminder of the lamb killed at the first Pesach.

Green vegetable
It is usually lettuce and/or parsley; it is dipped in salt water as a symbol of the tears slaves shed; it is also a symbol of spring (hope).

Charoset
It is a sweet paste made from apples, wine and nuts. This makes the Jews think about the sweetness of their freedom. It looks a bit like the mortar slaves used to hold the bricks together.

Bitter herbs
This is usually horse-radish which tastes so strong that it makes the eyes water; it reminds the Jews of the bitterness of slavery.

Activities

1. During the Seder, the Jews drink four glasses of wine to remember the four promises God made. What were they?
    (Clue: Exodus 6: 6-7 four reasons are given)
    a) Why is some of the food dipped in salt water?
    b) Why is matzah eaten?

2. The first Passover dates back to Moses about 3,000 years ago.
    a) Why do Jews recall this event today?
    b) How does this event show the importance of the family?
    c) Why is tradition important in modern life?

3. As well as in the synagogue, the practice of Judaism is centred in the home: for example, the blessing of food, the Sabbath meal.
    a) Identify ways in which Christianity is lived out in the home.
    b) In what ways do you think this influences behaviour and attitudes?

Know about the Exodus.
Reflect on the message it has for us today.

The Exodus

The story of the Exodus is one of the greatest events in the history of the Chosen People. It is about the weak and the powerless eventually winning – being victorious – because they put their faith in God. The Pharaoh had been warned in advance but he would not listen, his heart was hardened. The various plagues were a manifestation of the power of God. They showed that God is truly the Lord of history and no power on earth, no matter how great, could stand against Him.

True to His word, God guided and protected the Israelites as they left Egypt. But once they reached the banks of the Red Sea, they panicked. How were they going to get across?

Meanwhile, back in Egypt, the Pharaoh was having second thoughts. He led his army out to bring the Israelites back. With the Red Sea in front of them, and the Pharaoh's soldiers approaching from behind, the odds against them seemed impossible. Slaughter seemed inevitable.

Victory! Moses trusted in God. If God had promised to save and protect His people, God would not let them down. Sure enough, once again, the impossible became possible. Moses lifted his staff and the Red Sea opened and let them through and the waters closed behind them.

Use your Bible...

Read about the departure of the Israelites pursued by the Egyptians (Ex. 13:17-22; 14:1-31). Write down three key points to remember.

Signs of Rebellion

With mighty deeds and outstretched arm Moses brought the Israelites out of Egypt into the wilderness.

To start with, all went well for them: they sang songs praising God for setting them free. However, despite the wonders and miracles that they had seen God perform in Egypt – from the plagues to the parting of the Red Sea – the people's faith in God was still weak. Although they had placed their trust in Moses as God's representative, when the going started to get tough, the Israelites turned against him and blamed him for what they saw as their misfortune. They faced a barren, inhospitable land and, after travelling for three days, their water supply had dried up and they were thirsty.

They started to grumble to Moses saying that they had food to eat and water to drink in Egypt: **"As it is, you have brought us to this wilderness to starve this whole company to death!"** (Ex. 16:3).

God Provides

Moses must have felt really frustrated with these people. "Why don't you trust God?" he kept asking them. But then he prayed to the Lord and the Lord sent them food and drink. First, small plump birds known as quails fell from the sky, so the people had meat to eat. Then, they discovered a sweet kind of bread on the ground when they woke up in the morning; this was called manna. God also instructed Moses to strike a rock with his staff, and a stream of water flowed from it for the people to drink.

 Use your Bible...
Read the detailed account Ex. 16; 17:1-7.

 **Activities**

1. Imagine you are one of the Israelites and write a page in your diary.
   - Have you regrets about leaving the slavery in Egypt where you had food, shelter, routine?
   - Where is God now?
   - Is Moses up to the job?
   - Will we survive physical hardships in the desert?
   - Food comes, but will it come again?

2. Reflect on a time in your own life (or that of someone you know) when you left a safe but unhappy situation for the unknown. What were the worries, regrets and hopes for the future? Did help come and, if so, from where?

3. Choose any one of the Ten Commandments (on page 38) and prepare a 'Speech' to last no more than one minute.
   a) Explain why it is important.
   b) State what the consequences may be if we choose to ignore it.
   c) Conclude with an attractive 'catch phrase' so that everyone will want to follow your advice.

4. Compare and contrast the people of the Exodus with refugees today.
   Think about:
   - why they are fleeing;
   - what they are seeking;
   - problems they face;
   - possible solutions.

Know about God's covenant with His Chosen People.
Reflect on what we can learn from it.

The Covenant with Moses

After three months in the wilderness, the people who were led by Moses reached Mount Sinai. God took the initiative to make a **covenant** with them. He said:

"You have seen what I did to the Egyptians, and how I bore you on eagles' wings and brought you to myself. Now therefore, if you will obey my voice and keep my covenant, you shall be my own possession among all peoples; for all the earth is mine, and you shall be to me a kingdom of priests and a holy nation" (Ex. 19:4-6).

The people responded: "All that the Lord has spoken, we will do!" They agreed to the covenant promises and Moses took their reply back to God (Ex. 19:8).

The Ten Commandments

God told Moses about the Law which the Israelites were to follow. Its moral and spiritual demands were summed up in the Ten Commandments (Ex. 20).

1. **I am the Lord your God. You shall not worship false gods instead of me.**

2. **You shall not take the name of the Lord your God in vain.**

3. **Remember to keep holy the Sabbath.**

4. **Honour your father and your mother.**

5. **You shall not kill**

6. **You shall not commit adultery.**

7. **You shall not steal.**

8. **You shall not bear false witness against your neighbour.**

9. **You shall not covet your neighbour's spouse.**

10. **You shall not covet your neighbour's goods.**

Pause to Reflect

Are the Ten Commandments for us? Let's think about it.

Deep down within us, in the most private and secret part of our hearts, God speaks to us through our conscience. This is where we listen to God. (Cf. CCC 1776)

Through listening to God we will discover that living close to Him is the way to find true inner peace.

When we look into our conscience we find that we already know, without any one teaching us, that some things we do are good and will help us come closer to God. But we also find some things are not good and will never lead us to God or make us happy.

Think of the Ten Commandments as a way that leads to God and to happiness. This is what God intended for the Israelites and for all of us.

Activities

1. a) Which of the commandments could be applied to life in school?
    b) If everyone lived them what would life be like for:
    - pupils;
    - caretakers;
    - teachers?

2. 'Covenantal goods are non-zero-sum games, meaning, if I win, you also win.' Work in pairs: Give examples to show how keeping each commandment has a 'win win outcome'.

3. 'The Ten Commandments are out of date.' Discuss.
   a) Say what you **think** and **why**.
   b) Give a different point of view and say why some people hold it.
   c) Say why you **disagree** with it.
   d) Quote some source of evidence.

The Covenant is Sealed

God had taken the initiative to bring together the scattered people of Israel. He chose them to be **His own** people when He said, **"Now you will be my people and I will be your God"**. All the people said, **"We will observe all the commands that God has decreed"** (Ex. 24:4).

Then Moses put all the commands of the Lord into writing and built an altar to the Lord. This **covenant** was sealed with the blood from an animal sacrifice, poured out on an altar and scattered over the people.

Faith Tested – Promises Broken

Once again, the faith of the Chosen People was put to the test. They were left alone for forty days when God asked Moses to come to Him:

"Come up to me on the mountain and stay there while I give you stone tablets of the Law and the commandments" (Ex. 24:12).

During the forty days, while Moses was with God, the people grew restless. They started to doubt. They did not know what had happened to Moses and they quickly forgot the promise that they had made: **"All that the Lord has spoken we will do!"** They decided to turn back to pagan gods and made a statue of a calf as an image of a god. It was moulded out of gold and they started to celebrate, holding a great feast in honour of this so-called 'god'.

When Moses eventually came down from Mount Sinai carrying God's commandments on two stone tablets, and saw the people dancing before the calf, he was furious. He shattered the tablets and ground their golden calf into dust.

God threatened to send a plague. God said to Moses:

"I can see how headstrong these people are! Leave me, now, my wrath shall blaze out against them and devour them; of you, however, I will make a great nation" (Ex. 32:9-10).

But Moses pleaded with God: **"Leave your burning wrath; relent and do not bring this disaster on your people"**. Moses reminded God of the covenant He had made with Abraham and his descendants. So God relented and did not bring the disaster upon them.

Activities

1. In groups: write a script for a role-play of Moses challenging the people and the excuses they offered.
   - How do you think Moses helped them to understand the gravity of their sin?
   - What arguments do you think he used to help them repent?

2. In what ways do we make our own gods today? Choose one of the following and explain.
   - Sports;
   - Celebrities;
   - Music;
   - Money.

WHO

WHAT   WHERE

WHY   WHEN

3. 'Israel's idolatry only differs in form from what people worship today.' Prepare for a debate. Work in pairs. Draw an outline of two hands.
   a) Using 'On the one hand' and 'On the other hand' try to come up with arguments for and against the statement:
   b) Form your own conclusions. Try to give examples to back them up.
   c) In two groups debate the statement.

Know that God sent the prophets to remind the people of His covenant and unfailing love for them.
Reflect on the message of the prophets for us today.

God's Justice

In order to understand God's love for His Chosen People and for us, we need to understand His justice. God wants what is best for us. He is *like* a very good parent who will **warn you of risks** you are taking if you make a wrong decision or neglect your duty, for example, if you waste your time at school. The parent has more experience of what life is like as an adult and knows how important it is to have good qualifications.

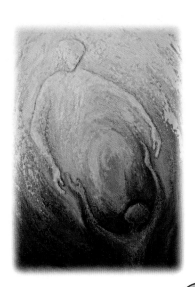

God is *not like* a parent who nags and tries to force you to do something against your will. He will not impose Himself on you. If you choose to ignore Him and say I don't want your good advice or your love, He will respect your freedom!

Pause to Reflect

What do you think it is like for God when people break their promise and choose to ignore Him?
- How do you feel when people make promises and think nothing of breaking them? Do you trust them again?
- What is your reaction when people you have really trusted betray you; when they go off with others and act as if you no longer existed?

Promises Broken

Time and time again the Chosen People broke their promises. They were human as we are. When life was comfortable and they had all they wanted, many of them tended to forget about the One who provides. From the time they reached the Promised Land, their history was recorded as a time of growing infidelity. God was always faithful to His promises. He looked after His Chosen People with great mercy and compassion but they took everything for granted. As long as they were able to get on with their own lives, they behaved as if they didn't need God.

The Prophets Message of Hope

Like a good parent, God sent prophets to warn the Chosen People of their infidelity. The prophets' message was fierce when they encountered people who believed they had no need of God, but they also had a message of hope.

Jeremiah

Through the prophet Jeremiah, God said: "For I know the plans I have in mind for you – it is Yahweh who speaks – plans for peace, not disaster, reserving a future full of hope for you" (Jer. 29:11).

"Behold, days are coming," declares the LORD, "when I will make a new covenant with the house of Israel and with the house of Judah, not like the covenant which I made with their fathers in the day I took them by the hand to bring them out of the land of Egypt. They broke that covenant of mine so I had to show them who was master. It is Yahweh who speaks" (Jer. 31-33).

Activities

God is talking to the people of Israel through the prophet Jeremiah, but God's message is true for us today.
a) What signs of hope do you see in the world around you?
b) What assurances do we have that God will keep His promises?

Take time to think about it.

Ezekiel

Through the prophet Ezekiel God said:
"This is the covenant which I will make with the house of Israel after those days," declares the Lord. "I will put my law within them, and on their heart I will write it; and I will be their God, and they shall be My people" (Ezek. 36:24-27).

"I am going to take you from among the nations and gather you together from all the foreign countries, and bring you home to your own land. I shall pour clean water over you and you will be cleansed; I shall cleanse you of all your defilement and all your idols. I shall give you a new heart, and put a new spirit in you; I shall remove the heart of stone from your bodies and give you a heart of flesh instead. I shall put my spirit in you, and make you keep my laws and sincerely respect my observances." (Ezek. 36:31-34)

Activities

The prophet Ezekiel said that God will remove the heart of stone from our bodies and give us a new heart of flesh instead.
Compare and contrast the ideas in this prophecy.
This could be in the form of a diagram of two hearts.

What do the prophecies mean?

With Moses, the law was written on tablets of stone. It was ratified or sealed with the blood of animals. Now, the time was coming when God would make a **new covenant**, but instead of it being on tablets of stone it would be written on the people's hearts:

"I will put my law within them and on their heart I will write it".

God was going to put **His Spirit** into His people. It would no longer be a set of external rules to be observed but the presence of God's Spirit within each person.

Activities

1. Watch the Power Point presentation on the prophets. (DVD ROM)
   a) Choose a sentence or two from either Jeremiah or Ezekiel.
   b) Think of a way to illustrate the meaning of it.
   c) Explain what it teaches about God's covenant.
   d) What impact is it likely to have on the Chosen People?

2. Work in groups. Discuss the difference between a set of rules to be observed and your conscience telling you what is right and wrong?
   Give examples to explain the difference

Understand that Jesus has come and will make a New Covenant with us.
Prepare to celebrate the birth of Jesus.

Preparation for the coming of Jesus

It became clear that while the Israelites tried to live according to the Law of Moses they needed help. They yearned for a life of intimacy with God. God did not forsake those who wanted to remain faithful to Him. He sent prophets with a message of HOPE.

The prophet Isaiah foretold:
"Behold a young woman shall conceive and bear a son and shall call his name Emmanuel " (Is. 7:14).
This name means God-with-us.

Advent for Mary

Mary was a young girl. Her relationship with God was extremely important to her. She was always seeking to do His will so she was ready when God came into her life.

God sent the angel Gabriel who greeted Mary as "full of grace" or "highly favoured one". Mary is "greatly troubled": there must be some mistake here; she knows herself to be the simple, humble maidservant of the Lord. "Do not be afraid, Mary, it is you who have found favour with the Lord". And when she is told that she "will conceive and bear a son who will be called the Son of the Most High", she is utterly amazed.

Mary asks, "How can this be (that I have a son), since I have no relations with men?" Once again, she is reassured that God and God alone will do it all: "The Holy Spirit will come upon you, and the power of the Most High will overshadow you; therefore, the child that will be born of you will be called Son of God." Mary responded in absolute faith, she freely let God take over in her life: "I am the maidservant of the Lord; let it be done to me according to your Word". Mary gave God a real, serious chance in her life.

 ## Pause to Reflect

What are the two most important lessons we can learn from Mary?

Advent for us

The season of Advent starts four weeks before Christmas. It is a time for us to grasp and understand more deeply the most amazing truth of all:

- God came to earth.
- He came to save us from sin.
- He came to seek and save the lost.

However, for many of us, our lives are so cluttered, we are busy, we have television, computers, Internet, iPods, etc.. Frequently, we move from one thing to the next like robots. We are full of our own likes and dislikes and – there is no room for God!

For many weeks, the high streets are illuminated and shops windows glitter with all kinds of things to convince us that we really must have them. In the lives of many, the Christmas rush is on, shopping, parties, presents, cards clutter lives. Is it preparation for 'Happy Holiday' or 'Happy Christmas'?

Activities

1. Plan an interview with the manager of a high street store that has the greeting, 'HAPPY HOLIDAY' in the windows. Your aim is to encourage him/her to replace it with 'Happy Christmas'. Think deeply before you write!
    Reflect on the difference between the two greetings.
    - What impact are they likely to have on the shoppers?
    - What effect is 'Happy Holiday' likely to have on family life?
    - How is this shift in emphasis likely to affect our country?

2. a) Meeting the Manager: role-play in groups of four, two take the part of the manager and his assistant and the other two interview them. Both groups need to take minutes of the meeting.
    b) Give a report of the meeting to the rest of the class.

The Birth of Jesus: God among us

When the appointed time came Mary "gave birth to her first-born son and wrapped him in swaddling clothes, and laid him in a manger, because there was no place for them in the inn".

Read the account of the Nativity in your Bible, Luke 2:1-20 and take time to reflect on each sentence.

Activities

1. Imagine you are one of the shepherds. You have been entrusted with the Good News. What will you do with it now?

2. Design a double-bubble map to show the true meaning of Christmas and how to prepare for it.

Jesus makes a New Covenant

At Christmas, we celebrate the birth of Jesus. This means that God became human so that human beings could come back to God. The covenants that God made with our ancestors in the Old Testament were a preparation for the new covenant which is fulfilled in Jesus.

In the Mystery of the Eucharist and the Paschal Mystery which we will go on to study, Jesus has made this **new covenant** with us. It is in and through this **new covenant** that Jesus has opened the way to heaven for us and for all people who earnestly seek to love God and love their neighbour.

Preparation for Jesus coming again!

If Jesus has already been born in Bethlehem, how can we still look forward to him coming?

The Church teaches that Jesus **will come again**. Jesus will come again at the end of time to bring about the final fulfilment of His Father's loving plan of liberation from pain and suffering; salvation for all who earnestly seek it and eternal happiness with God. The early Christians always met every week on a Saturday night and spent the time in prayer and contemplation on the readings from the Scriptures. They made an all night vigil to celebrate the Eucharist in the early morning. They were preparing for the real, final coming of Jesus.

So our **Advent** and **Christmas** are a **'remembering'** of the past coming of Jesus in his incarnation and birth but we also **'get ready'** for the real *future* coming of him at the end of time. However, we will not be ready with open hearts for the future final coming of Jesus, unless we practise *in the present* to keep our hearts open for the daily coming of Jesus, who really comes to us in the persons, events and circumstances we meet every single day and every moment of every day.

> "Have you not heard his silent steps?
> He comes, comes, ever comes.
> Every moment and every age,
> Every day and every night
> He comes, comes, ever comes.
> Rabindranath Tagore, Gitanjali

Activities

1. The poet tells us that Jesus comes to us every moment of the day.
   a) In what ways does Jesus come to us today?
   b) What clues did Jesus himself give us? Read Mt. 25:35.
   c) In what ways would the world be a better place if we truly recognise Jesus among us?

2. Make a thinking map for this Advent to help you
   a) remember the past coming of Jesus;
   b) prepare for his future coming;
   c) recognise the daily coming of Jesus into our lives through:
      • people *(Think about people who need your help)*
      • events *(Are they opportunities to thank God, to ask for help, to offer help?)*
      • circumstances. *(Do they challenge us to get out of self-love, self-will, self-pity?)*

3. Mystery of the Eucharist

Understand that Jesus is our Saviour.
Think about what this means for us.

A Mystery

What is a mystery? It has several meanings: something hidden, difficult to fathom, unknown, even exotic! But these are not the meanings that the Church gives to the word 'mystery'. The theological meaning of the word 'mystery' is a divine reality which has been revealed in a visible form. It is something which comes from God for our salvation. Jesus knew that it would be very difficult for people to understand this so he used a very human situation to help them grasp its meaning.

One day, when thousands of people followed him to a hillside Jesus knew the people were hungry and had nothing to eat. He wanted to show them that he could *not only* satisfy their **physical needs** for food but also their **spiritual needs**. This is where we begin to explore the meaning of the mystery of the Eucharist.

Feeding the Five Thousand

We join the disciples who are with Jesus on a hillside. It is shortly before the Jewish feast of Passover; crowds of people have followed them. Jesus said to Philip, **"Where can we buy some bread for these people to eat?"** Philip told him that there was a small boy with five barley loaves and two fish, but he knew that would not go very far. There were more than five thousand people!

When Jesus blessed the five loaves and two fish there was plenty for everyone. When they had eaten enough he said to the disciples, **"Pick up the pieces left over, so that nothing gets wasted"**. So they picked them up and filled twelve baskets with the scraps left over.

The people, seeing this sign that he had given, said, "This really is the prophet who is to come into the world" (Jn. 6: 1-15). They were intrigued and went looking for him again the next day.

Jesus knew why they came and said to them:
"I tell you solemnly,
you are not looking for me
because you have seen the signs
but because you had all the bread you wanted to eat.
Do not work for food that cannot last,
but work for food that endures to eternal life..." (Jn. 6:26).

The people didn't understand and asked, "What sign will you give us to show that we should believe in you? What work will you do? Our fathers had manna to eat in the desert..." Jesus explained that it was not Moses who gave them bread but God. So they asked him to give them that bread always (Jn. 6:31). By their question they showed, not only that they did not understand, but that they were missing the point altogether!

Use your Bible...

Read the Miracle of the Loaves (Jn. 6:1-15; 22-58).
What did Jesus really want the people to understand?

Activities

1. a) Study this clip art image, copy and complete it.
   b) Give it a title and write your explanation of the image.

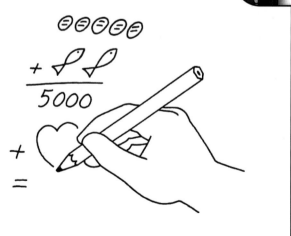

2. a) What do you think Jesus meant when he said, 'Do not work for food that cannot last, but work for food that endures to eternal life'?
   (Clue: Think about what Jesus wanted them to understand.)
   b) Does this still apply to us today? Give reasons.

Jesus, the Bread of Life

The following teaching of Jesus is not for the 'faint-hearted', it is tough so you need to be ready for strong words!

Jesus explains what the food is that gives eternal life:
"I am the bread of life.
He who comes to me will never be hungry;
He who believes in me will never thirst.
But, as I have told you,
You can see me and still you do not believe".

"Your fathers ate the manna in the desert
And they are dead;
But this is the bread that comes down from heaven,
so that a man may eat it and not die.
I am the living bread which has come down from heaven." (Jn. 6:35-36;49-51)

Pause to Reflect

Watch the Power Point presentation where Pope Benedict XVI explains what Jesus meant when he said, 'I am the bread of life'.
Make notes on what it means for you.

Intolerable Language

The Jews started arguing: "How can this man give us his flesh to eat?" they said. Jesus replied:

"I tell you most solemnly,
if you do not eat the flesh of the Son of Man
and drink his blood,
you will not have life in you.
Anyone who does eat my flesh and drink my blood
has eternal life,
and I will raise him up on the last day.

For my flesh is real food
And my blood is real drink.
He who eats my flesh and drinks my blood
lives in me
and I live in him" (Jn. 6: 53-57).

After hearing this many of his followers said, "This is intolerable language. How could anyone accept it?" It was too much for them; many of his disciples left him.

Then Jesus said to the Twelve, **"What about you, do you want to go away too?"** Simon Peter answered, "Lord, to whom shall we go? You have the message of eternal life, and we believe; we know you are the Holy One of God" (Jn. 6:67-69).

It was difficult for the disciples and it is very difficult for us to understand what Jesus said. Many of the Jews were scandalised at his words, they thought it was 'cannibalism'. Jesus did not take back what he said. He even repeated and emphasised that he really does mean his flesh and blood as food and drink. It is the body of Jesus offered out of love as a sacrifice that takes our sins away.

Pause to Reflect

What would you have said if you were there? Why?

What does this really mean?

This is where we make the link with the Eucharist – the Eucharist is a true meal, but not any kind of meal. It is a sacrificial meal: **"the bread that I shall give is my flesh for the life of the world".**

It helps to remember that this is a mystery. A mystery we will never fully understand but one which we can ponder and, with the gift of faith, one in which we believe.

Activities

1. Imagine you were one of the disciples with Jesus when he spoke to the people. The following day you are stopped by a journalist. He has heard that strange things have been happening and wants to get an article for his newspaper. Think carefully before you answer his questions.

   Journalist:
   - Excuse me; you were with the prophet from Nazareth on the hillside.
   - Can you explain what happened there?
   - What do you think this Jesus was trying to say?
   - What gives him the authority to say such outrageous things?
   - Do you still consider yourself one of his followers? Why?
   - Do you think he will get his large following back? Why?

2. Work in small groups to produce the newspaper article for the journalist. Remember to include the opinions of the group but be sure you include the true disciples who remained faithful to Jesus. Use your ICT skills.

> **Understand the New Covenant Jesus makes with us.**
> **Reflect on our part in this New Covenant.**

The New Covenant

In the next chapters, we will be studying in depth our participation in the New Covenant through the mystery of the Eucharist and the paschal mystery. We are now going to explore how it began.

How did this New Covenant take place? We know that God sent His only Son, Jesus, to us. In other words, God took on our human nature and became man. Because Jesus was truly God and truly human, he was in a unique position to bridge the gulf between God and human beings when he gave us the **New Covenant.**

The Last Supper

The twelve disciples never forgot the last Passover meal they had with Jesus. He told them how much he longed to celebrate this feast with them because this was to be the beginning of the New Covenant.

St. Paul tells us what happened.

"For I received from the Lord what I also delivered to you, that the Lord Jesus on the night he was betrayed took bread, and when he had given thanks, he broke it, and said, **'This is my body which is for you. Do this in remembrance of me.'** In the same way, after supper, he took the cup saying, **'This cup is the new covenant in my blood. Do this, as often as you drink it, in remembrance of me'.**

For as often as you eat this bread and drink the cup, you proclaim the Lord's death until he comes." (1Cor. 11:23-26)

Pause to Reflect

What do you think is the most precious gift that Jesus has given to us?
Where and **when** do you think Jesus wants you to receive this gift?

What does the New Covenant mean for us?

Jesus was not asking his disciples just to consecrate bread and wine in remembrance of him. What Jesus is saying is: **"Do this, which I have done, in remembrance of me".** On the night when Jesus was betrayed, he freely handed himself over, that is, he gave his life in love to the Father. He said "This is my body which **is handed over for you.** Do this in remembrance of me." He is now asking us to hand over ourselves in love to him and by helping one another.

Our way to the Father had been closed because of our selfishness and sin. Through his death and resurrection, Jesus handed over himself in love for us; it is this that opened a new way to the Father for us. This was the New Covenant. The choice is now ours to enter into this New Covenant relationship with him; that is to hand over our lives in love to him and love one another as he has loved us. In return, he promises us eternal life and everlasting joy with him in heaven.

Activities

1. Think about all that you have seen, heard and believe about the Last Supper and the New Covenant. Explain how it gives meaning and purpose to the lives of many Catholics.
   Think about:
   - what they believe;
   - how their belief affects their lives;
   - where they draw strength and courage;
   - examples.

2. The covenant is made when the people accept it and undertake to fulfil their part of it.
   a) What is the covenant that Jesus has made with us?
   b) What is the part that we have to fulfil? Give examples.

3. "Look after yourself; nobody else will." Discuss this statement in the light of your study of the New Covenant.
   Think about:
   - your beliefs and values;
   - beliefs and values generally held in society today;
   - challenges.

Celebrating the Mass Today

Together We Meet Jesus

At the beginning of Mass, we come together to meet Jesus. The priest greets the people. His greeting, 'The Lord be with you', proclaims the presence of Jesus in the community gathered together.

The Penitential Rite

The priest invites the people to call to mind their sins, to repent of them and to ask for forgiveness. The following poem is to help us to reflect on how words can hurt.

Truth
Sticks and stones may break my bones,
But words can also hurt me.
Sticks and stones break only skin,
While words are ghosts that haunt me.

Slant and curved the word-swords fall
to pierce and stick inside me.
Bats and bricks may ache through bones,
but words can mortify me.

Pain from words has left its scar
On mind and heart that's tender.
Cuts and bruises now have healed;
it's words that I remember.

Barrie Wade

We are asked to examine the way we behave towards God and towards each other. Can we say that we have truly loved God and loved all the people with whom we have come in contact? Frequently, we fail to live up to this great command of Jesus. So, at the beginning of Mass, we are invited to call to mind our sins and ask for God's forgiveness.

When we have received God's forgiveness we should be ready to forgive others. This is not always easy, so in our hearts we ask God to give us the grace to help us to do it.

Pause to Reflect

Re-read the poem 'Words that Hurt', reflect on these questions.
   a)   How can words be ghosts that haunt us?
   b)   How can words be swords that hurt?
   c)   What sort of scars is the poet talking about?
   d)   How can scars be healed?

Sin Separates
Forgiveness Unites ...

A strange thing happened on Christmas Eve in 1937. A middle-aged man, who worked as a labourer, went to visit an elderly lady at the house of a priest. He was very upset and begged the woman to forgive him; she assured him that she already had done so. Read the facts below.

Maria Goretti died in 1902 at the age of eleven. She was the victim of a young man's rage. When she resisted his advances, the man, Alessandro Serenelli, stabbed her fourteen times. She died later in hospital, but before her death she said, "May God forgive him, because I have already forgiven him". The murderer, who was still in his teens, was sentenced to thirty years in prison.

The middle aged man was Alessandro Serenelli; the elderly woman was Assunta Goretti, Maria's mother. They later went to Midnight Mass together at a church containing a shrine to Maria Goretti.

Activities

1. Alessandro could have waited until Mass was over before he met with Assunta. Why do you think he did not do this? The answer is in the 'Our Father'.
Pick it out and write it down.

2. Why do you think the Penitential Rite happens early in the Mass? (Clue Mt. 5:23-24)

3. Have you ever had an experience of being loved and accepted after doing something that was wrong? Describe your experience.

Pause to Reflect: A True story

This is a story of a nun who lived in an American city. There, after many years teaching, she took up a job as a worker for the diocese, helping people to understand justice and peace in their lives.

After some time of illness her doctor told her that she had cancer and needed chemotherapy, which involves chemicals being put into the body to destroy the cancer cells. Each week she went to the hospital for treatment. It worked well. She got better; the cancer was destroyed. On her last visit, when she was receiving her last infusion of chemicals, she looked around the waiting room at all the very sick people, including some children. She felt fine and she thanked God that she had been cured. At 10.30 am she returned home. At 11.00 am the phone rang. It was the hospital.

They asked her to return immediately. She drove back there, puzzled. The hospital administrator and her medical consultant met her and took her into his office. They told her there had been a terrible mix-up. She had been given another person's mixture of chemicals. Slowly, she asked if it was a serious mistake. Even more slowly, they explained that it was, in fact, a fatal mistake. The mixture she had received would cause her death. There was nothing that could reverse it. She was stunned. Then she asked how long the process would take. When would she die? "In about six hours," they said.

Sister was devastated; she wept for quite some time. Gradually, she became more composed. When they asked if there was anything she wanted, she began to speak. She asked first to see the nurse who had made the mistake. When he came he was in tears. She told him not to be too upset. "I've made many mistakes myself," she said. "It's easily done; though none has had these consequences." Then, she asked him to remember that it was, in some ways, providential that it had happened to her and not to someone else. "After all," she said, "as a religious Sister, I do not have a husband or children. It might have been much worse." She also said that her whole life was centred on Jesus and that she was ready to go, through death, to meet him. That was what she had lived for.

Then, she asked for a video camera to be brought. She spoke in front of the camera, making a film of messages for her community, her brothers, their children, her friends. She had no time to see them again.

By this time it was 1.30 pm so she asked for her Religious Superior to come and the Archbishop. Everyone was in tears. She asked the Archbishop to celebrate Mass, there in the room. Together, with the doctor and the nurse, they prayed together, received Holy Communion and asked for the strength of God's grace.

It was now 3.00 pm and the Sister was beginning to feel weak and ill. She was taken to a private room and was put to bed. She went to sleep.
At 4.00 pm she woke. Quietly she whispered her last wish to her Superior and to the Archbishop.
She made both of them promise not to take any action against the nurse or against the hospital. She wanted them to make sure that the same mistake didn't happen again, but that was all. No blame; no compensation; no retribution. She was at peace, and ready.

At 6.00 pm she died.

Activities

1. Make an emotional chart to show the feelings of the nurse:
   a) when he discovered he gave the wrong injection;
   b) when the Sister forgave him;
   c) that night when he was alone.

2. a) What is the most important message in this true story?
   b) How do you think the Sister's daily attendance at Mass helped her in this crisis?
   c) How did she live out the 'handing over of herself' at Mass?
   d) How does this story show that she had inner freedom?

3. Share with the person next to you what has impressed you most about the 'True Story'.

Know that the Bible is the Word of God.
Think of ways in which you can put the Word of God into practice.

The Liturgy of the Word

What does the Word of God mean? We believe that the Bible is God's Word. It is God speaking to us. God has spoken to us for a very long period up to when Jesus became man. Jesus was then called the Word. "The Word was made flesh" (Jn. 1:14).

When we listen to the readings from the Bible, we are hearing God speaking directly to us. We listen carefully in order to know how to put His teaching into practice in our everyday life.

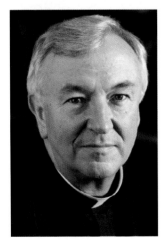

The readings are not just a record of what happened long ago. We believe that the Bible **is** God's Word. We don't say, 'This **was** the Word of the Lord'. We say, 'This **is** the Word of the Lord'. We believe God is speaking to us through these words now, so we try to listen with our hearts.

This is what Archbishop Vincent Nichols does. He says: "I just try to hear one phrase or one sentence, and I think, 'Oh that's helpful'. I try to remember it, to hang on to it. It might be that I am upset; it just gives me a bit of comfort. I think God uses these words to get through to me. And that is why I think we also say, 'This is the Word of the Lord' now, for you and for me, each time we go to Mass".

Here are some examples:

"Love your enemies, do good to those who hate you, bless those who curse you, pray for those who treat you badly" (Lk. 6:27).

"Judge not, and you will not be judged; condemn not and you will not be condemned; forgive and you will be forgiven; give and it will be given to you; good measure, pressed down, shaken together, running over, will be put into your lap" (Lk. 6:37-38).

"If anyone loves me he will keep my word, and my Father will love him, and we shall come to him and make our home with him" (Jn. 14:23).

"Do not let your hearts be troubled. Trust in God still, and trust in me" (Jn. 14:1).

Activities

1. Think about recent events in school. Consider how listening to the Word of God at Mass might influence our behaviour and the way we treat each other.

2. Imagine one of the above examples from scripture were given in a reply to an 'Agony Aunt' letter in a Christian magazine. Write out the original letter which provoked this answer.

3. Write a scene for a 'soap' that communicates one of the five scripture quotations above.

4. a) Draw up a code of behaviour based on the scripture quotations above. Ask for it to be discussed at the student council meeting for adoption in the school.
   b) Put it into practice for two weeks and note the effect it has on the class.
   c) Appoint a group to write a report and present it to the school council or head teacher to be considered when the behaviour policy is reviewed.

The Offertory

At the Offertory, when we see people taking the bread and wine up to the altar, we should imagine we are walking up with them and offering our whole life to Jesus. In the two symbols of bread and wine, it is as if we are bringing all the parts of our life and placing them on the altar. Jesus then takes them as part of his offering, so we are offered to the Father with him.

At this part of the Mass the priest prays quietly on our behalf:
"By the mystery of this water and wine we come to share in the divinity of Christ, who humbled himself to share in our humanity".

"Lord God, we ask you to receive us and be pleased with the sacrifice we offer you with humble and contrite hearts".

This offering does not happen automatically. When we enter the church we have to be conscious of what we are doing and freely make this offering of ourselves each time we go to Mass. What happened at Calvary almost 2,000 years ago is made present today.

The gift of ourselves and all we do to help others, God transforms into something beautiful. In return, we receive God's love and grace to help us to grow close to Him and to experience inner peace.

> "When I got home from school I gave my mum a hug and asked her about her day. I helped her wash up and cook and I sent a text message to my sister to wish her a happy Valentine's Day. That day I felt relaxed when I went to bed because I didn't get as worked up as I usually do because I tried my best to think of things in the way Jesus would deal with them in each situation.
> I went to bed with a light, 'anger-free' head!
>
> Next day I woke up in a good mood after my nice sleep. I was calm and concentrated in class – normally, sadly enough I am very talkative and loud. I helped to separate my friends who were having a fight instead of standing there and doing nothing. These are small things but I know I have been trying to live like Jesus and can make this offering at Mass."
>
> Nunya

I started to be a fully committed Christian when I came back from school and I really felt like a new person. First thing I did was to vacuum and dust. Then, I helped my dad fix some things around the house because we had just moved house.

Samuel

Activities

1. a) What preparation do you think should take place in school before the celebration of Mass?
    b) How can an individual prepare for Mass?

2. Explain the significance of the Offertory.
    Think about:
    - the words and actions of the priest;
    - our thoughts and actions;
    - God's response.

Know that, at the Consecration, Jesus becomes truly present on the altar. Think about what this means to you.

The Consecration

What does the Consecration mean?

At the Consecration, Jesus becomes truly present to us in the bread and wine which is changed into his body and blood.

This is the heart of the tremendous mystery. This is the way in which God reaches out to us. He gives Himself to us in the gift of Jesus, who is truly God and truly man.

How do we know this happens?

We know it only by faith. At the Last Supper, when Jesus gave the bread to the apostles he said 'This is my Body'. When he gave them a cup of wine to drink he said, 'This is my blood'. Then he said, 'Do this in memory of me'. Jesus can bring about what he says.

At Mass the priest says these same words. He says them 'in the person of Jesus Christ'. They are truly spoken at each Mass as they were at the Last Supper. The bread and wine cease to be bread and wine. **They become the body and blood of Jesus. 'Do this in memory of me' is not just remembering what Jesus did; it means that we have to hand over ourselves in love as Jesus has done.**

How is this miraculous change brought about?

It is brought about through the power of the Holy Spirit. It was the Holy Spirit who, at the command, or word, of the Father, brought about creation. It was the same Spirit that raised Jesus from the dead. This same Spirit acts again in response to the words of Jesus as they are spoken by his Church, in the person of the priest.

Pause to Reflect
Watch the Power Point presentation 'The Last Supper'. Take time to reflect on the questions at the end of it.

The Truth

THE WAY, THE TRUTH & THE LIFE SERIES

At the Consecration
We remember and we participate in the Last Supper which Jesus had with the apostles before he was crucified. Jesus gave them bread and said:

"This is My Body".
In other words Jesus was saying, 'This is me, really and truly present'.

Then Jesus gave each of the apostles the cup of wine to drink and said:

"This is my blood".

Jesus was saying, 'This is me, really and truly present'.

After that, Jesus said:

"Do this in memory of me'.

What does this mean?

- Jesus hands himself over in love to his Father;
- Jesus hands himself over to us in the Eucharist;
- He asks us, in remembrance of him, to hand over our lives to the Father and to hand over our lives in love and service to one another.

We believe the words of Jesus because we believe that he is God. We still see bread, we still see wine, but with our faith we say, this is Jesus really and truly present.

Pause to Reflect

- The fact that Jesus is really and truly present in the Eucharist is the most powerful and most challenging belief that exists for Catholics today.

- What does your faith tell you? Reflect deeply about it on your own.

- What difference does this belief make to your life?

- Our faith is like a tiny seed; every day we must plead with God to make it grow.

Activities

1. a) What would you consider to be the most valuable treasure on earth?
       Why?
    b) What steps would you take to attain this treasure?
    c) How does your answer compare with the Gift that is offered to us in the Mass? Think deeply before you answer.

2. Work in pairs.
   What do you think could be done to help people understand the true meaning of the Consecration? Think of two suggestions to share with the class.

Jesus made the Perfect Sacrifice

In the Old Testament, the high priest offered the blood of an animal as a sacrifice, but Jesus gave himself, his own body and blood. When Jesus freely offered his life on the cross, he gave himself in love to the Father as the most perfect sacrifice to take away the sins of the world.

At Mass, the same sacrifice that Jesus made on the cross on Calvary is made present again **'in mystery'.** That means that Jesus is truly present but under the sacramental sign of bread and wine.

At Mass, when the priest says, **'Let us proclaim the mystery of faith'**, this mystery is a truth too big for our minds to grasp. It is the mystery of the sacrifice of Jesus made truly present for us, but under the sign of bread and wine.

Pause to Reflect

What does the above illustration suggest to you?

Our Self Sacrifice

Jesus' offering of himself can only be understood by a person with faith and a heart that loves. We are asked to live out the words of Jesus: to love one another as he has loved us. We are asked to **hand over our lives.**

We have to put aside:
- self-love;
- self-pity;
- self-interest;

and to seek ways to be:
- helpful;
- thoughtful;
- kind;
- generous.

Every time we make an effort to help others, it is as if Jesus is saying to us: **"Come, you whom my Father has blessed … For I was hungry and you gave me food I was thirsty and you gave me drink …."**

We might ask, but when did we do this?
"I tell you solemnly, in so far as you did this to one of the least of these brothers of mine, you did it to me" (Mt. 25:35 & 40).

Liz shares her experience of finding ways to help others:

"I really found it hard today. I was helping my mum as much as I could: preparing the table, washing up the dishes, helping with the dinner, cleaning the house, helping my brother with his homework, weeding the garden and putting my brother to bed which is a real hassle. After all that, I felt exhausted and my feet wouldn't move an inch. Now, I know what my mum must feel like after a whole week and here I was complaining just after one day!
Then I thought – what about the sacrifice that Jesus has made for me!"

Pause to Reflect

- Think about the sacrifices your parents make for you.
- Reflect on the efforts you already make to help others.
- Think of what you could do this week.

Activity

Fr. Maximilian Kolbe, a prisoner in the concentration camp in Auschwitz in 1941, is an example of someone who offered his life to save someone else.

a) Watch the Power Point presentation on him.
b) Explain the similarities and differences between the sacrifice Jesus made and the sacrifice made by Fr. Maximilian Kolbe.

Know that when we receive Holy Communion,
Jesus is truly present in the form of bread and wine.
Consider how we should prepare for this occasion.

Holy Communion

When the priest repeats the words that Jesus said at the Last Supper: **'This is my body, this is my blood',** the bread becomes Jesus' body and the wine becomes Jesus' blood. We still see bread and wine – but in faith we believe Jesus is present.

Before Jesus gave his life for us, eternal life with the Father was closed to us because of our sin and selfishness. Through his death and resurrection Jesus **handed over himself in love for us; it is this that opened a new way to the Father for us.** It is through Jesus that we go to God.

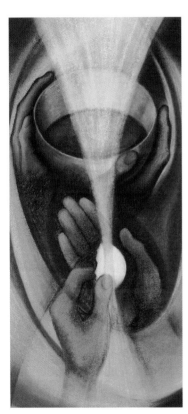

Receiving Holy Communion

We share fully in the sacrifice of Jesus Christ by receiving his body and blood in Holy Communion. When we receive the host, it is not bread we receive: it is the body of Christ present in the form of bread. When we receive from the chalice, it is not wine we drink: it is the blood of Christ present in the form of wine. When we receive Christ in Holy Communion, we become more deeply part of him, and so we are given a promise of sharing his life fully in heaven.

When we receive Holy Communion we know, by faith, that it is Jesus Christ we receive. We welcome him into our hearts. The time after Holy Communion, then, is a time of most special prayer. During it we speak personally to Jesus who is present within us.

St. Teresa of Avila tells us what happens when we receive Jesus in Holy Communion:

"He shows Himself to those whom He sees will make good use of His presence, although they do not see Him with their physical eyes. He has many ways of showing himself to the soul with great interior feeling and through other means. Stay with Him, with an open heart.

What's more, if we don't take any notice of Him but we go away from him as soon as we've received Him, to seek other more down-to-earth activities, what can He do? Has he got to drag us by force to see Him if He wants to make Himself known to us?

Don't waste this perfect moment – the time after Holy Communion – for being with Him. If, after having received Him your mind is full of other things and you don't take any notice of Him, nor even realise that He is in you, how is He going to make Himself known to you?"

Activities

1. a) Use bullet points to summarize what St. Teresa says happens when we receive Holy Communion.
    b) On a card, write a reflection to help focus your thoughts when you receive the Eucharist.

2. Watch the Power Point presentation 'Jesus present in the Eucharist' in which Pope Benedict replies to a question about Holy Communion. Make a summary of the main points.

Reflect on how we can live out the Mass in our daily life.

"Go in peace to love and serve the Lord."

No other event past, present or to come, can match the cosmic event that takes place in our churches all over the world each time Mass is celebrated. What happened physically over 2,000 years ago happens now in the mystery of the Eucharist when Jesus is truly present.

When we go to Mass, we do not go as **observers** to look on at what is happening, we go to **hand over ourselves to Jesus**. This is because each one of us has been redeemed by Jesus: that means that he has opened the way to the Father for us. The choice is now ours to accept this WAY to the Father.

What does this choice involve? It means we have to strive daily to live our lives for Jesus. He was willing to give his life for each one of us. He is now asking us to be ready to follow his way; that is, getting out of thinking about our own needs and noticing the needs of those around us and doing something about them.

Pause to Reflect

Read the Gospel of Matthew 25:31-40: "For I was hungry and you gave me food". Take time to meditate on it.

Living it out!
Christina decided to live out this scripture text for twenty-four hours:

My first act as a radical Christian was to give up my time to help someone. After school I stayed with Adjoa to help her for an hour. At home, I cleaned up (something I don't often do). I did everything I was asked to do, including lending my sister some money for the shops. At break time next day, I gave away almost a whole packet of custard creams (my favourite biscuits). At the end I felt fulfilled, encouraged and had a sense of spiritual healing.

Activities

1. Take time to reflect. Commit yourself to twenty four hours of living as a fully committed follower of Jesus. Write down what you did and how you felt at the end of it.

2. Sometimes young people say they are bored at Mass. This is because they don't understand what is happening and what they need to do. Your mission now is to help other pupils in your school understand the Mass.
   Work in pairs. Design a section for the school website or make a booklet for Year 7 pupils who are new to the school.
   Explain what happens at:
   • the Penitential Rite;
   • the Liturgy of the Word;
   • the Offertory;
   • the Consecration;
   • Holy Communion;
   and how we live out the Mass.

3. Write an imaginary email to someone you know who no longer goes to Mass on Sundays.
   • Explain what you now understand about the Eucharist.
   • How it has challenged and/or helped you to appreciate what happens at Mass.
   • Make some suggestions that you think might encourage this person to return to Mass.

4. We don't go to Mass as observers, but to participate.
   Give five examples of how to participate at Mass.

4. The Paschal Mystery

I wonder what's in it for me.

What's in it for us?

Sometimes, our first thoughts when we are asked to do something are to consider what will we get out of it or what it will do for us, maybe even, 'Why should we?' or 'We'll do it if ...'.

This is not unlike what two of the disciples said to Jesus:

"James and John, the sons of Zebedee, approached him. 'Master,' they said to him, 'we want you to do us a favour.' Jesus said to them, 'What is it you want me to do for you?' They replied, 'Allow us to sit one at your right hand and the other at your left in your glory'. 'You do not know what you are asking,' Jesus said to them. 'Can you drink the cup that I must drink?'" (Mk. 10:35-38)

Here Jesus was explaining to them that to be a close friend of his, it was not a matter of being granted favours but of following his example of total self-giving.

As we now approach the climax in the life of Jesus, we will understand in a new way what this involves.

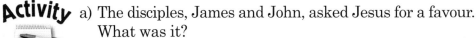
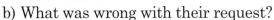

Activity
a) The disciples, James and John, asked Jesus for a favour. What was it?
b) What was wrong with their request?
c) What might be some of the favours you could or should ask Jesus for? Why?

Holy Week: The Most Important Week in the Year

Every year, Christians all over the world re-live the events which happened over 2,000 years ago. They re-trace the steps of Jesus during the last week of his life on earth, day-by-day, sometimes hour-by-hour, for a whole week. It is known as **'Holy Week'** and it lasts from Passion Sunday to Holy Saturday. This is how it began.

Use your Bible...
Triumphant entry into Jerusalem
Read Mark 11:1-11.
Note the mood of the crowds in verses 8 and 9.

Jesus' friends
thought that he was going to be triumphant once they reached Jerusalem. But Jesus himself knew that the only way he could bring us totally to God was to suffer and to die. Even though pain, humiliation and death lay ahead, Jesus was determined. This was God's will and he would fulfil it.

EXPECTATIONS

Religious leaders felt
threatened and challenged by Jesus.

Political leaders believed
Jesus was a threat to the nation. It was time he was tried for treason.

We ourselves
have to face troubles in our lives. Sometimes, we have to suffer for things we know are right or have to be done. But we have the example of Jesus to follow, and the knowledge that he is always there to give us strength and help us.

The people came out in droves to cheer for Jesus, the miracle-worker because they wanted him to overthrow their oppressors. They expected Jesus to lead an uprising of military and political liberation, not to lay down his life as a spiritual sacrifice for Romans as well as Jews!

Activities

1. What do you think Jesus would have wanted to say to each group? Think carefully before you write each one and make your own diagram of the replies.

2. a) Watch the Power Point presentation of what happens in church on Passion Sunday.
   b) Compare and contrast this liturgy with Mark 11:1-11.

Deepen our understanding of the events of Holy Thursday. Reflect on the importance of this day for us.

Holy Thursday

Several memorable things happened at the Last Supper that Jesus shared with the twelve disciples. One disciple slipped away. The others wondered why. They thought he'd gone out to get something. The truth was Judas had decided to betray Jesus. He had accepted some money to tell the authorities where Jesus would be at a quiet time and how they could arrest him.

Pause to Reflect

Read and reflect on John 13:1-15. Jesus washes his disciples' feet.

At the Last Supper, Jesus washed his disciples' feet. They were shocked at this! By doing this, Jesus was trying to get a very important message across to them which was that his role was to serve others and not to be served. Peter tried to stop him, but Jesus explained why he was doing it. He was not just performing an act of kindness; he was doing the work of the lowest servant. He did not claim any status for himself or high position of Lord and Master. This is why Jesus said:

"I have given you an example so that you may copy what I have done" (Jn. 13:15).

St. Paul explains that even though Jesus is God, while he was on earth **"He did not cling to his equality with God, but emptied himself** (of his status as Son of God) **to assume the condition of a slave..."** (Phil. 2:6-7).

Jesus is not asking us to wash each other's feet, but rather to put our own selfish interests aside and to provide for the needs of others.

 Activity

1. A Night to Remember
   Imagine you were with the apostles at the Last Supper and had your own ideas about what you thought would happen.
   In bullet points describe and explain:
   · what your expectations were;
   · what you witnessed;
   · what you want to remember and why;
   · the impact this experience is likely to have on your life.

2. Watch the Power Point presentation of Mass on Holy Thursday.
   Using your knowledge about the Jewish celebration of the Passover, what is different and what is the same about this night's celebration?

3. Holy Thursday is a very special day in the Church's year.
   Why do you think this is so? Think deeply.

The Garden of Gethsemane

After the last supper, aware that Judas was about to betray him, Jesus left with his disciples to go to the Garden of Gethsemane on the Mount of Olives. There, he became deeply distressed and troubled. "He withdrew from them, about a stone's throw away and knelt down and prayed. **'Father,'** he said **'if you are willing, take this cup away from me. Nevertheless, let your will be done, not mine'."**

Then an angel appeared to Jesus, coming from heaven to give him strength. In his anguish, he prayed even more earnestly and his sweat fell to the ground like great drops of blood.

When he rose from prayer he went to the disciples and found them sleeping. **"Why are you asleep?"** He said to them. **"Get up and pray not to be put to the test"** (Lk. 22:39-46).

Jesus knew what lay ahead of him; he willingly accepted it. But here in the garden, he felt totally alone.

His disciples had fallen asleep. He had asked Peter, James and John to watch and pray with him, but they too were asleep. There was no one around. Jesus knew what was going to happen. He knew that Judas was bringing the Temple guards to arrest him. He knew that this would result in his being condemned to suffering beyond human endurance. His words to his Father, **"If it is possible take this cup from me?"** shows the anguish he was going through.

At this time, Jesus was being tempted to get up and walk away. BUT he accepted the inevitable, and said **"not my will but yours be done".** It is through prayer that Jesus gained strength to fight the temptation to run away. And it is through prayer that he gained the strength to follow his Father's will.

 Activity
a) What do you think caused Jesus to suffer most grievously?
b) Explain in your own words the nature of the struggle Jesus experienced.
c) How did he respond?

Pause to reflect on people suffering today.

Cardinal Basil Hume tells us that there are no quick answers to the problem of suffering. "The mystery of God is too great and our minds too small, too limited to understand His ways. But I cannot, and will not, doubt the love of God for every person, a love that is warm, intimate and true. I shall trust God, even when I find no human ground for doing so." (The Mystery of the Cross p.12)

Activity

1. a) Think about a time when you have been scared, lonely, or you have not wanted to do something that you knew you should.
   b) What can you learn from Jesus' experience that might help you in the future?

2. Watch the Power Point presentation of the Altar of Repose on Holy Thursday.
   a) Why do you think it is important to stay alone in prayer for a little while at this Altar?
   b) Why do some people stay there till midnight?

Good Friday

The hour had come to arrest Jesus. "Judas, one of the Twelve, came up with a number of men armed with swords and clubs, sent by the chief priests and the scribes and the elders. Now the traitor had arranged a signal with them. 'The one I kiss,' he had said, 'he is the man. Take him in charge and see he is well guarded when you lead him away.' So when the traitor came, he went straight up to Jesus and said, 'Rabbi!' and kissed him.

The others seized Jesus and took him in charge. Then one of the bystanders drew his sword and struck out at the high priest's servant, and cut off his ear.

Then, Jesus spoke. 'Am I a brigand' he said 'that you had to set out to capture me with swords and clubs? I was among you teaching in the Temple day after day and you never laid hands on me. But this is to fulfil the scriptures.' And **they all deserted him and ran away"** (Mk. 14:43-51).

Activities

1. What do you think motivated Judas to betray Jesus?
   Do you think he had thought it through? Why?
   What do you think he might have expected would happen?

2. a) Describe what you understand about 'BETRAYAL' and give examples.
   b) When could it be right to divulge information?

The Trial before the Sanhedrin

The armed men led Jesus off to the high priest; and all the chief priests and the elders and the scribes assembled there.

Use your Bible ...
Read Mark 14: 55-65 slowly and carefully.
Look to see if the following rules are observed.

Rules for Trials:
• Jewish trials had to be held during the hours of daylight.
• Two independent witnesses had to agree on their evidence, if not the defendant had to be acquitted.
• The High Priest sat in judgement but could not ask any incriminating questions.

Activities

1. Do you think the Sanhedrin followed the rules above? Give reasons using the scripture text to help you.

2. Work in groups. Each group divides into Teams A and B.
   a) Prepare for a discussion on the following:
      Team A: Write down as many reasons as you can why the Jewish authorities considered Jesus guilty or a threat.
      Team B: List reasons why Jesus should have been released because he was innocent.
   b) Based on the evidence of the groups would you have freed Jesus or declared him guilty?
      Give reasons for your answer.

Peter's denials

While Jesus was being tried by the Sanhedrin, Peter was in the courtyard. One of the high priest's servant-girls came along, stared at him and said, "'You too were with Jesus, the man from Nazareth'. But he denied it. 'I do not know, I do not understand, what you are talking about' he said. Peter went out into the forecourt. The servant-girl saw him and again started telling the bystanders, 'This fellow is one of them'. But again he denied it. A little later the bystanders themselves said to Peter, 'You are one of them for sure!' He denied it again. At that moment the cock crew for the second time, and Peter recalled how Jesus had said to him, 'Before the cock crows twice, you will have disowned me three times'. And he burst into tears" (Mk. 14:66-72).

Pause to Reflect

- Why did Peter say he didn't know Jesus?
- Why was he such a coward?
- Think of how he must have felt when he heard the cock crow.
- Are there times when we have good intentions and then find ourselves doing the exact opposite?

Activity

a) Read Matthew 27:3-9.
b) Compare and contrast the actions of Peter and Judas when they realised what they had done.

The Sequence of Events:

- **Many had been celebrating the Passover meal the previous evening.**

- **Jesus and his disciples had gone to a secluded garden after the Passover meal.**

- **Jesus had been arrested in the garden.**

- **The disciples had run away and hidden themselves.**

- **Jesus had immediately been taken and tried in the house of Caiaphas the High Priest.**

- **Jesus had been found guilty of blasphemy.**

- **Early in the morning shortly after sunrise, the Jewish authorities had brought Jesus to Pontius Pilate, the Roman Governor.**

The Trial before Pontius Pilate

At festival time, Pilate used to release a prisoner for the people, anyone they requested. Pilate asked them if they wanted him to release the king of the Jews because he realised that it was out of jealousy that the chief priests had handed him over. But the chief priests had encouraged the people to demand the release of Barabbas instead. Barabbas was a Zealot and had committed murder during an uprising. When Pilate brought both of these men forward, he asked the crowd who they wanted released. They shouted, 'Barabbas!' They called for Jesus to be crucified. 'Why?' Pilate asked them, 'What harm has he done?' But they shouted all the louder, 'Crucify him!' So Pilate, anxious to please the crowd, released Barabbas for them and, having ordered Jesus to be scourged, handed him over to be crucified (Mk. 15:14-15).

It seems very strange that, only four days previously, Jesus had been welcomed into Jerusalem with shouts of praise, palms being waved and cloaks being laid on the floor in front of him. Suddenly, the crowd was now calling for his execution and the freedom of a murderer!

Activities

1. a) Read the account of the trial in Matthew 27:11-26.
   b) Explain the conflicting considerations that led to Pilate's verdict.
      Think about:
      - Pilate's wife;
      - his duty to the Emperor;
      - the responsibility of his job;
      - the pressure from the Sanhedrin;
      - the emotion of the crowd;
      - the impression Jesus made on him.
   c) What was the final verdict? Do you agree with it? Give reasons for your answer.

2. Listen to the audio recording 'From the house of the High Priest'. (DVD ROM) Imagine you were there. Write a page in your diary to record events.

3. Plan an assembly for the school. You may wish to use:
   Meditation on the Way of Sorrows (Audio recording DVD ROM)
   Choose a hymn; write prayers of intercession and a closing prayer.

The Death of Jesus

It is virtually impossible for us to imagine the suffering that Jesus experienced on Good Friday.

His friends had deserted him.

He had been beaten, whipped and crowned with thorns.

People spat in his face in front of the crowd.

He had a heavy, wooden, rough cross forced on him and been made to carry it to Calvary.

He had been stripped and nailed to that cross.

And now, he was hanging there, with people all around insulting him, waiting for him to die.

Thief
I too, was nailed to a cross. 'Jesus,' I said, 'remember me when you come into your kingdom.'

Onlookers
We thought he was the Son of God – our hopes are now shattered!

Mary
The nails and sword went through me as I watched my son die on the cross.

Peter
I was hiding a good distance off when I heard my master cry out: "My God, my God, why have you forsaken me".
What did it mean, had God forsaken him?

You?

Although he was God, Jesus was also fully human. As he hung on the cross, he felt thirsty. A soldier offered him bitter vinegar. After he had taken the vinegar he said, **"It is accomplished"** and bowing his head he gave up his spirit and died (Jn. 19:30).

"It is accomplished!" Those words are so simple and yet so powerful. Jesus is dead but, by dying, he has completed the task that he set out to complete. The journey has reached its end.

Activities

1. a) Watch the Power Point presentation on the Stations of the Cross. (DVD ROM)
   b) Work in pairs. Each pair takes a 'station' and relates it to an experience or event in life today. (Suggestions on DVD ROM)

2. Jesus suffered in many ways: physically, emotionally, psychologically.
   a) From what you have studied, give an example of each type of suffering.
   b) What type of suffering do you think was the hardest? Why?
   c) In what ways does Jesus continue to suffer in people today?

3. a) Watch the Power Point presentation on Good Friday in church.
   b) Describe and explain the meaning of this liturgy.

4. How does the suffering and death of Jesus influence Christians today? Think about:
   • those who suffer physically, mentally, psychologically;
   • what the death of Jesus accomplished;
   • how it inspires people.

5. Classroom Discussion.
   Why is the suffering and death of Jesus important to Christians?
   Study the statements which your teacher will place around the room. (Statements on DVD ROM)
   a) Tick on the statement that is closest to your opinion.
   b) Work in groups. Decide on the three most important reasons.
   c) Share them with the class and reach a consensus.

Holy Saturday: A time of deep silence!

Disciples

The disciples experienced the silence of God.
It appeared as though God had been defeated.
Their Lord and Master had been killed.
The previous day, they had been stunned into silence by one unforeseen event following another.
They must have felt ashamed because they had disowned their Lord.
They saw themselves as traitors and cowards.
Their hopes of a future with him had come tumbling down.
They spend Holy Saturday in fear and dread that something worse was coming.

Mary

Mary reflected on what had happened. She held on to the total trust she had in God's promises. Even though her heart must have been pierced with suffering she was able to instil hope into the confused disciples. She remembered all that God had done for her and hoped in Him.

Mary spent Holy Saturday in trust and patience contemplating the mystery of God's plan.

Ourselves

In the disciples we see the confusion, bewilderment and fear that we sometimes feel when we cannot find God and wonder if He really exists.
Mary teaches us how to be faithful.
She believed completely in God's plan and teaches us to do the same, even though, like her, we cannot see into the future.
Mary teaches us to trust in God at all times, especially when we are going through something very difficult, such as being abandoned by friends or our family breaking up.

Activities

1. Imagine you are Mary. It is the Sabbath (Holy Saturday) and all is quiet.
   Your son is dead, killed as a criminal.
   You are all alone except for John.
   Write a poem to express your feelings.

2. a) Watch the Power Point presentation of the Easter Vigil in church.
   b) Design a leaflet: 'My Guide to the Easter Vigil'. Include symbols and explanations to show all you understand about it.
   Think about:
   - lighting of the fire and paschal candle;
   - what the symbols on the candle mean;
   - why the congregation light small candles from the flame of the paschal candle, (make reference to Mt. 5:14-16);
   - renewal of baptismal promises.

**Deepen our understanding of the meaning of the Resurrection.
Reflect on its importance for us.**

The Resurrection

The day of rest, the Sabbath, had passed. Dawn broke. Daylight started to fill the sky. People could once again resume their daily business.

Pause to Reflect

Even though it is not recorded in the Gospels, we may assume that Jesus first appeared to his mother, Mary.
It is highly likely that she was still praying and pondering over all the events that had taken place.
Imagine Jesus coming to her.
What do you think he said?
What do you think it was like for Mary?
How did it help her to understand all that had happened in her life?

The Empty Tomb

"Jesus is alive and we have seen him!"

This was the most sensational news that the disciples had ever heard. Two days had passed and now they were astounded by the news that Mary of Magdala had brought to them. She had seen a vision of angels who declared:

"He is not here: For he has risen as he said!" (Mt. 28:6)

The disciples reacted in different ways. Peter and John rushed to see for themselves. Others waited in disbelief until Jesus appeared to them that evening.

Doubting Thomas

"Thomas, called the Twin, who was one of the Twelve, had heard the news, but he was not with them when Jesus came. When the disciples said, **'We have seen the Lord'**, he answered, **'Unless I see the holes that the nails made in his hands and can put my finger into the holes they made, and unless I can put my hand into his side, I refuse to believe'**.

Eight days later, the disciples were in the house again and Thomas was with them. The doors were closed, but Jesus came in and stood among them. **'Peace be with you'**, he said. Then he spoke to Thomas, **'Put your finger here; look, here are my hands. Give me your hand; put it into my side. Doubt no longer but believe.'** Thomas replied, **'My Lord and my God!'** Jesus said to him: **'You believe because you can see me. Blessed are those who have not seen and yet believe'**" (Jn. 20:24-29).

The writers of the Gospels list numerous occasions after the resurrection when Jesus appeared alive and real to his followers, for example, in the garden itself, in the upper room, on the road to Emmaus and at the Sea of Galilee.

Activities

1. Imagine that the news of the resurrection of Jesus has spread around Jerusalem but the guards cannot find him. All who claim to have seen him are rounded up and brought to court to be questioned. You are among them.
   a) Divide into six groups. One group will be the guards and all the others eye-witnesses.
   b) The eye-witnesses must study their scripture text very carefully and be prepared to be questioned by the guards.
   c) The guards must decide the questions they are going to ask based on Matthew 28:11-15.

Group 1 Mary of Magdala
(Jn. 20:1-18)

Group 2 Peter with an eyewitness
(Jn. 21:9-17)

Group 3 The disciples on the road to Emmaus
(Lk. 24:13-35)

Group 4 The apostles gathered together
(Lk. 24:36-43)

Group 5 The disciples on the shore of Tiberias
(Jn. 21:1-14)

The Jury
When your group is not being questioned by the guards you are the jury.

Judge
The teacher will sum up the evidence and decide on the verdict.

The Power of the Resurrection

The appearances of the Risen Jesus had such a profound effect upon the disciples that, shortly after the resurrection, they devoted their lives entirely to telling people that:

- **Jesus died for our sins;**
- **Jesus rose from the dead;**
- **Jesus will come again.**

The resurrection gives us **HOPE** that death is not the end.

Death was NOT the END for Jesus and it is NOT the END for us.

Jesus' resurrection broke the power of sin and this gives us HOPE because we know that GOOD will triumph.

The disciples followed Jesus' instructions by celebrating the Eucharist together, sharing bread and wine and knowing that it had now become his Body and Blood.

The Catechism of the Catholic Church tell us that: "United with Jesus Christ by Baptism, believers truly participate in the heavenly life of the risen Christ, but this life remains 'hidden with Christ in God'. The Father has already 'raised us up with him, and made us sit with Him in the heavenly places in Christ Jesus'. Nourished with his body in the Eucharist, we already belong to the Body of Christ. When we rise on the last day we 'also will appear with him in glory' (CCC 1003).

"Christ will raise us up 'on the last day; but it is also true that, in a certain way, we have already risen with Christ. For, by virtue of the Holy Spirit, Christian life is already now on earth a participation in the death and Resurrection of Christ." (CCC 1002).

**Activities**

1. Imagine that you were present when Jesus appeared after the resurrection, for example, you could be
   Peter (Jn. 21:1-18)
   Mary of Magdala (Lk. 24:1-11)
   Cleopas (Lk. 24:13-35)
   Thomas (Jn. 20:19-29)
   Nathanael (Jn. 21:1-17).

   a) Say who you are and what you were doing when Jesus appeared.
   b) What did he say?
   c) What did you do as a result?
   d) What effect did it have upon your belief in Jesus and your life afterwards?

2. "By rising from the dead on Easter Sunday, Jesus provided the ultimate proof that there is life after death - and all of us share in it." Discuss.
   a) Say what you **think** and **why**.
   b) Give a different point of view and say why some people hold it.
   c) Say why you **disagree** with it.
   d) Quote some source of evidence.

5. The Mission of the Church

Deepen our understanding of the Church.
Reflect on what it means for us.

Challenges to Christianity
Newspaper Headlines

BISHOPS FEAR NEW BILL COULD FORCE SCHOOLS TO TAKE DOWN CRUCIFIXES

Catholic schools and care homes could be forced to remove crucifixes and holy pictures from their walls in case they offend atheist cleaners, bishops have warned MPs.

NURSE SUSPENDED FOR OFFERING TO PRAY FOR PATIENT

ORDER TO REMOVE CRUCIFIX

Necklace posed a 'health and safety risk' in hospital.

Over to You

Most likely you have been studying Christianity for several years. Have you paused to reflect on what it means to you personally? Does it really matter? Are you ready to be challenged by others who reject the existence of God?

Many people will have heard of the Catholic Church but may have little understanding or a very narrow view about it. Does it matter? Why?

The reality is that we are living in a society where secular humanism is challenging Christianity. The secular humanists reject the existence of God and the supernatural. They claim that moral issues, such as abortion and euthanasia can be decided by people as best fits their needs.

As Christians, we hold firmly that all human life is sacred; life originates with God; human beings are both physical and spiritual and made in the image of God. From the moment of conception every human being has an inherent God-given value.

It is vital for us to be aware of what is happening and not let Christianity be undermined. We have to know what the Catholic Church teaches and understand why this teaching is rooted in the values of Jesus Christ. For this reason, the mission of the Church involves every baptised Christian. We are all called to be missionaries. God has created each one of us to have a particular part in His plan of salvation.

Activities

A few years ago, atheists had the following advert put on buses:

"There's probably no God. Now, stop worrying and enjoy your life".

Draft a reply to the British Humanist Association who sponsored this advert. Explain what belief in God means to you and others you know; how it affects your behaviour and the quality of your life.

What is the Church?

If you ask people to define the Church you are unlikely to get the same answer from any of them. Here are a few examples:
- a unique place for religious worship;
- a place of quiet where I can go;
- a quiet place where I can talk to God and He will listen;
- a community of people;
- a teaching authority.

One reason why it is difficult to explain the meaning of the Church is because it is a mystery of faith. We have to think deeply and look for several meanings in order to understand the different aspects or images of the Church; some of them are not obvious. It is not like a mystery that is hidden or unknown; it is a divine mystery which has been revealed and some aspects of it can be seen. It belongs to God, but for our salvation it has been revealed to human beings.

The Church is the People of God

Once we were nobody, now we are a people whom God called "out of darkness into His own wonderful light". The light we live in is the knowledge that we have been chosen, loved and redeemed by Jesus. Jesus has given us our new identity. Why? So "that we may declare the wonderful deeds of God" (1Pet. 2:9-10).

What does it mean for us?

First, we need to know that our roots are in the Old Testament. We know that God took the initiative to use Moses to lead His own people out of Egypt and that he made a covenant with them.

However, now there is a *new* covenant which God has made in and through His own son Jesus. Moses had sealed the covenant with the blood of an animal, but Jesus made the *new* covenant with his own blood. Jesus handed over his life in love for us. Jesus has given us a new identity – **we are his chosen people**. With our new identity Jesus has given us a New Commandment with two parts to it. The first is, "You shall love the Lord your God with all your heart, and with all your soul, and with all your mind". And the second is like it, "You shall love your neighbour as yourself" (Mt. 22:37-39).

The Church is the Body of Jesus Christ

"There is one Body, one Spirit, just as you were all called into one and the same hope when you were called. There is one Lord, one faith, one baptism, and one God who is Father of all, over all, through all and within all. Each one of us, however, has been given his own share of grace, given as Christ allotted it." (Eph. 4:1-7)

What does it mean for us?

When St. Paul explained that the Church is the Body of Jesus Christ, he wanted to stress that, while different gifts are given to a variety of people, there is only one Spirit. So he said that, just as the human body has different parts to it and each part has a different function, the body remains one single body. So in the Body of Christ, which is the Church, there are many gifts given to us, but the Spirit is one, and the Church, which is the Body of Christ is one.

It helps to think of it as Jesus, the Head and, the Church as the Body. It is the Head that makes life flow into the Body.

Through the Sacrament of Baptism we become members of the Body of Christ, the Church.

The Church is a Community

Just as the human body counts on each cell to do its part, so the Body of Jesus Christ counts on each of us to do our part. St. Paul said, "If one part of the body suffers, all the other parts suffer with it" (1Cor. 12:26).

Jesus came to heal, to serve, to reconcile, to bind up wounds. He is the one who comes alongside us in our sorrow and joy. He died that we might live. He has risen from the dead so that we, too, may have eternal life with him in heaven.

What does it mean for us?

"Everything the true Christian has is to be regarded as a good possessed in common with everyone else. All Christians should be ready and eager to come to the help of the needy . . . and of their neighbour in want. A Christian is a steward of the Lord's goods" (Catechism of the Catholic Church 952).

Pause to Reflect

"When someone steals another's clothes, we call them a thief. Should we not give the same name to one who could clothe the naked and does not? The bread in your cupboard belongs to the hungry; the coat hanging unused in your closet belongs to the one who needs it; the shoes rotting in your closet belong to the one who has no shoes." St. Basil

 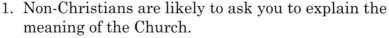  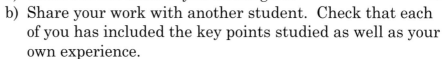

Activities

1. Non-Christians are likely to ask you to explain the meaning of the Church.
   a) Write out the answer you would give.
   b) Share your work with another student. Check that each of you has included the key points studied as well as your own experience.

2. *A little fellow in a ghetto was teased by one who said, "If God loves you, why doesn't he take care of you? Why doesn't God tell someone to bring you shoes and a warm coat and better food?" The little fellow thought for a moment; then, with tears starting in his eyes, said, "I guess God does tell somebody, but somebody forgets."*

   Discuss: What message does this have for each of us?

**Understand the Mission of the Church.
Reflect on what it involves.**

What is the Mission of the Church?

To understand the mission, we need to understand the reason for it. God created the world out of love, but things went wrong and people distanced themselves from God's love and from one another. God made a covenant through Abraham, Moses, David and the prophets to bring about that relationship of love and open the way to salvation. Finally, God came to earth in human form as Jesus, to show us how to live lives pleasing to God. Jesus taught us about God's love, which is for all people, no matter who they are. Jesus showed forgiveness, justice and compassion to all. He re-established the right relationship with God through his life, death and resurrection.

Jesus was on a mission from God. Before returning to his Father, he passed on his mission to his disciples and through them to the Church:

"Go therefore and make disciples of all nations, baptising them in the name of the Father and of the Son and of the Holy Spirit, teaching them to observe all that I have commanded you; and lo, I am with you always, until the end of time." (Mt. 28: 19-20).

We need to continue this mission with God's Spirit living within us. People today search and yearn for God's love, forgiveness, salvation, justice and compassion.

In the next few weeks, we will be reflecting on the variety of ways in which people are living-out the mission of the Church, for example:

o **JUSTICE** for the poor;
o **COMPASSION** for the weak;
o **REPENTANCE** and **FORGIVENESS** among those who do wrong;
o **RESPECT** for human dignity;
o **FAITHFULNESS** to God and to His commandment.

Activities

1. Work in pairs. Think of an imaginative way of presenting the following information.
   a) What was Jesus' mission?

   | Lk. 4:18-19 | Mk. 1:15 |

   b) What mission did Jesus give to the disciples?

   | Mt. 28:18 | Lk. 9:1-3 |

   c) What is the mission of the Church today?

   | Jn. 13:34-35 | Rom. 12:6-8 |

2. a) Work in pairs. Choose one of these issues:
   * justice;
   * compassion;
   * repentance and forgiveness;
   * respect;
   * faithfulness.
   b) Share where you think this issue is most needed and give reasons.
   c) Design a flyer to promote it.

**Understand the importance of living out the teaching of Jesus.
Reflect on the work of the SVP.**

Blessed Frederic Ozanam

Through his own experience, Frederic Ozanam, a student at the Sorbonne University in Paris, understood the wisdom of St. Francis: 'Preach always, and if necessary use words'. One day, he was speaking in defence of the Church in a very lively debate at the university. He was challenged by other students: "What are you doing for the poor now? Show us your works!" Frederic realised that talk alone would be no good, he had to put the teaching of Jesus into practice, to live it out or it would not make sense to non-believers. That same night, together with a few friends they pooled what money they had and bought firewood for a poor family.

From that time onwards, this small group of students began to live the Gospel by showing love for their neighbours in need. They visited those living in dreadful poverty and brought them food and comfort.

Frederic was highly intelligent and became a professor at the university and still continued with others to meet the needs of as many people as possible. In 1833, he formed what is now known as the SVP, the St. Vincent de Paul Society, named after St. Vincent de Paul who had worked among the poor and oppressed in the 17th Century.

Frederic Ozanam was beatified on 23rd August 1997 by Pope John Paul II.

Activity

"Preach always, and if necessary use words".
St. Francis of Assisi
   a) What do you think this means?
   b) Why do you think St. Francis of Assisi gave this advice?
   c) Do you agree or disagree?
      Give reasons for your answer.

The St. Vincent de Paul Society Today

Feeding the hungry and homeless: members are involved in soup runs and in running day-centres for the homeless.

Clothing the naked: many groups have a clothing store. This enables them to provide good quality clothing and footwear for people in need.

Visiting the sick: members visit the sick in their own homes and also in hospitals, particularly those who have no one to visit them.

Children's Camps: for those who would not otherwise have a holiday.

Caravan holidays: for needy families.

Supporting elderly, housebound people: by visiting, shopping and arranging appointments for them.

Other Community Support Projects are too numerous to mention but they include support centres, furniture stores and hostels.

Opportunities for Schools

Youth SVP gives young people in secondary schools and parishes an opportunity to help and support other people. Many aged between 11-18 have contributed to voluntary work in their local community as member of a Youth SVP group.

How to get started:
Step 1: Find a Group Adviser
The group adviser would act as a support for the Youth SVP and would take responsibility for it.
Step 2: Contact the National Youth Development Officer.

"Joining the SVP makes the journey of faith into a great adventure. Members receive far more than they can ever imagine." Jessica

"We have the opportunity to reach out to those who need a listening ear and a helping hand." Matthew

Youth SVP

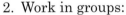
Activities

1. Find out where parishes and schools have a Youth SVP. Go to www.youthsvp.org.uk and click on 'Where do we work?' Put the cursor slowly over the dots on the map to find the centre nearest to your school or parish.

2. Work in groups:
   a) List some of the needs that an SVP group could meet in your local area.
   b) Give reasons why a group may or may not be necessary in your school.
   c) Share with the rest of the class and try to reach a decision.

3. Which image of the Church on pages 90-91 best fits the work of the SVP? Put the image in the SVP box and give reasons for your choice. *(See worksheet in TB or on DVD ROM).*

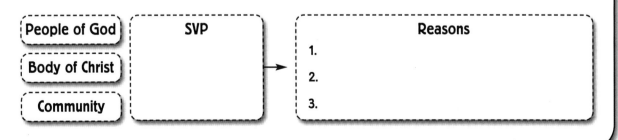

People of God	SVP	Reasons
Body of Christ		1.
		2.
Community		3.

Alberto Hurtado SJ

In Chile, South America, Alberto Hurtado is a hero, everyone has heard about him. There were no half measures for Alberto; he totally handed over his life to God and became the voice for the homeless.

Alberto was born in 1901 and his father died when he was only four years old. His mother was forced to sell the family house to pay their debts. Alberto had to live with relatives and often had to transfer from one to another.

As a young boy, he experienced the condition of one who
* **is poor;**
* **without a home;**
* **at the mercy of others.**

When he left St. Ignatius High School, Alberto studied Law at the Catholic university in the mornings. He worked in the afternoons and evenings to support his mother and brother.

Later, when he joined the Jesuits, Alberto studied theology and psychology in Belgium where he was ordained a priest in August 1933. The hardship he experienced as a child sharpened his sensitivity to the needs of others who were deprived and alone.

Alberto's Hurtado's Mission

Let us consider:
* what he saw;
* what he did;
* why he did it;
* what sustained him.

When he went back to Chile in 1941, he became very involved in helping the homeless, the street boys and girls at risk, those whom nobody wanted.

He fixed his gaze on Jesus and wanted to do his will.

It was only because he lived united to Jesus that Alberto could be an instrument in God's hands to work for others. He spent long hours in prayer and through this he could see **what to do**.

He started work immediately. He wanted homes where every homeless person would feel welcome.

Alberto had the knack for encouraging the well-off to loosen their purse strings to help the less fortunate. So with contributions from benefactors he opened a welcome house for young people, then for women and later for children. Alberto believed the poor are Christ Jesus. Five thousand homeless roamed the streets of Santiago.

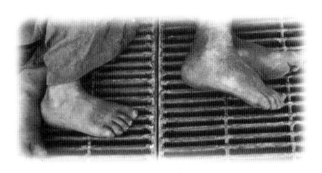

His burning desire was to gather them all in and give them love and an education. At night, he would go out in his little green van to find those abandoned. Many times he found children sleeping under a bridge by the river and would take them back to the home he had built, the **Hogar de Cristo**, the home for Christ Jesus.

In the daily celebration of Mass, Alberto united his heart to Jesus, who said, *"Whoever eats my flesh and drinks my blood remains in me and I in him"* (Jn. 6:56). Because of this, he could say, *"My Mass is my life, and my life is a prolonged Mass!"* His very close relationship to Jesus enabled him to give life to others. He lived the words of Jesus, "As long as you did it to one of my brothers, you did it to me" (Mt. 25:40).

Alberto firmly believed that Jesus made himself our neighbour or rather our neighbour is Jesus who reveals himself in people we meet: a patient among the sick, a needy man among beggars, a prisoner among the incarcerated, the heartbroken among those who weep. If we do not see him, it is because our faith is lukewarm. To separate our neighbour from Jesus is to separate light from light. He who loves Jesus is obliged to love his neighbour with all his heart, with all is mind, with all his strength. In Jesus Christ we are all one.

Alberto Hurtado died of cancer in 1952 and was canonised a saint on 23 October 2005.

Activities

1. a) Watch the Power Point presentation of St. Alberto Hurtado.
   b) Explain how his religious beliefs influenced his moral values and behaviour. Think about:
      - what he saw;
      - what he did;
      - why he did it;
      - what sustained him.

2. "My Mass is my life and my life is a prolonged Mass", Alberto Hurtado SJ. What do you think this means?

3. "We should not give money to the homeless in the streets because that only encourages them to be lazy." Discuss.
   (See worksheet on DVD ROM for guidance)

Understand the importance of helping people with disabilities. Reflect on how they can help us.

Jean Vanier

Jean Vanier, a man with a 'vision', put into action what Jesus said about inviting "the poor, the crippled, the lame and the blind" to share good things.

Having spent time in prayer and reflection on what God wanted him to do, he was convinced that God was calling him to establish a community for people with intellectual disabilities. He believed they were among the loneliest and most rejected in the world. He knew that the weak and the vulnerable were very dear to Jesus' heart. Some of them felt rejected by society because they were 'different', but to Jean, they were 'special', in them he saw Jesus.

He bought an old ruined house and called it L'Arche (The Ark). It opened on 5th August 1964 and became a warm, loving community for 'special' people. In a short time, he opened other L'Arche communities. There are now 117 of them in thirty-three different countries worldwide, spreading from Canada to the Ivory Coast, from India to Honduras, and from Great Britain to Haiti.

L'ARCHE

COMMUNAUTES FONDEES
PAR JEAN VANIER

Each L'Arche is a witness of God's love and care for those who are rejected or in pain. People no longer feel lonely because they are loved. They lead a very simple life in community: eating, working and praying together with time for celebrating and welcoming visitors.

Jean Vanier's vision was that the communities of L'Arche should be places where the gospel message is lived out, where people – no matter how handicapped or disadvantaged – should feel they were in the presence of Jesus, surrounded by others (a community) and the love of God. Most of all, they should be a place of welcome: *"Whoever welcomes one of these little ones in my name, welcomes me"* (Lk. 9:48).

Quick Quiz
What do you think the logo for L'Arche represents?

Pause to Reflect
In silence, read Fr. William's experience slowly and take time to reflect on it.

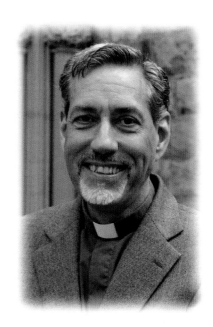

Fr. William Pearsall SJ recalls his experience with L'Arche soon after being ordained a priest. In 1987, he went to live with profoundly disabled people in Trosly – a farming village deep in the forest of Compiègne in the north of France. The farm houses all around are the 'foyers', or small communities of L'Arche. Fr. William admits he was a bit nervous about going there. "I was not at all attracted by the idea at first – I thought, No way! That's not me! It was only in prayer that I felt drawn, but it turned out to be – wonderful!"

Daily life at L'Arche is not at all starry-eyed or mystical. It is rooted in the very down to earth activities of washing, cooking, eating, cleaning, dressing, making beds, all the ordinary stuff of life. And it is built around people who are in pain, people with profound physical and mental disabilities – people who have been marginalised, excluded, broken, rejected – perhaps from very early on by their own parents.

From all this woundedness comes a pressing need for love, and the L'Arche community is formed around that need. For Fr. William, and for many young people who come to work at L'Arche from all over the world, the first response is pity and sadness. But then follows the miracle - **they discover that they themselves have the same needs and brokenness**. Indeed, this is the heart of Jean Vanier's message – we all experience pain, and rejection, and handicap. These are the basis of our common humanity, and L'Arche is a privileged place where we encounter 'humanity in the raw' – in others, yes, but just as profoundly in ourselves.

Fr. William looks back on his experience as a time of joy, of hospitality, of welcome, of discovering that the people he cared for, some with profound handicaps, were centres of life for the whole community. There is no place for power or violence or competition. Perhaps this is what the early Church was like! Everyone is called by their first name; no-one has special status – all are just friends together, sharing a common life. This includes, of course, sharing the tantrums and the tears as well, because what is being learnt here is *emotional* truth. It is a new experience for people who are used only to living 'in their heads'. This is an experience of relating 'heart to heart', at a level deeper than words.

To anyone thinking of joining L'Arche as an assistant Fr. William would say "It is life-changing for the young people who come as assistants! It was life-changing for me! But the only way to experience it is to go and see for yourself. It is like reading the New Testament – it's great, but in the end you have to live it and do it. L'Arche is a revolutionary way of living the Gospel. It is a living demonstration of how love works".

Activities

1. Explain the beliefs and values that inspired and influenced Fr. William during his time at L'Arche. Think about:
   - his initial reaction;
   - his own needs;
   - his discovery;
   - the contribution he made;
   - the overall value of the experience.

2. How did L'Arche help Fr. William or did he help L'Arche? Discuss.

3. How might these symbols summarise the mission of the Church in L'Arche?

4. In what ways do people with disabilities help us to live the mission of the Church? Think about the Church as the:
   - People of God;
   - Body of Jesus Christ;
   - Community.

Understand how the Taizé Community helps young people from over the world to live the Gospel. Reflect on why it is a powerful experience for them.

Brother Roger

Brother Roger was an amazing person. He was born on 12 May 1915 in Switzerland and was the youngest of nine children.

At university, he felt the call to monastic life but he was not sure what God was calling him to do. As a child, his grandmother used to tell him about how she assisted refugees during the First World War. This gave him a strong desire to help the poor and oppressed. He was also very conscious of the divisions between Protestants and Catholics and wanted to unite them.

In 1940, he left his home in Switzerland for France. On the way he came to Taizé, an almost abandoned village in Burgundy. It was the place for him to dream dreams and do something about them. He borrowed some money to buy a disused house and outbuildings and soon afterwards paid it back. He used this property to offer a welcome to political refugees and Jews fleeing the Nazi persecution. It was here that he dedicated his life totally to God and left his plans wide open for God to show him the way forward.

At first, he prayed alone, but in 1949, when he was joined by seven young men who wanted to commit their lives to God, he set up a monastic community. They became known as the Taizé Community and from the very beginning they have never accepted donations for themselves.

Taizé

Taizé has grown into an ecumenical community of over one hundred brothers where Catholics and Protestants live together and take monastic vows of poverty, chastity and obedience. It has become a centre of Christian unity in Europe. Once it was an insignificant hillock, but today it is like a mountain shining the torch of Christian faith for the rest of the world.

What is it like in Taizé?

The brothers offer hospitality. Numbers of visitors vary from a few hundred a week in winter time to over 5,000 at Easter and in the summer. They are mainly young people aged between seventeen and thirty. They come from about seventy-five different countries: Catholics, Anglicans, Protestants, Orthodox and evangelicals. These people come to explore or rediscover their Christian faith. They camp in fields around the church and monastery.

The programme is austere. There is one Catholic Mass celebrated at 7.30 each morning and then the daily routine is:

- Morning prayer
- Breakfast
- Large group bible study
- Small group discussion
- Midday prayer
- Afternoon work or bible study
- Discussion with the brothers
- Dinner
- Evening prayer and silence.

The bells chime three times a day, a call for prayer. In response, everyone moves towards the church which is a simple, cosy, quiet haven for souls.

The prayer consists mainly of short songs, repeated many times, such as:
Bless the Lord, my soul, and bless God's holy name.
Bless the Lord my soul, who leads me into life.

There is also a short reading from the Bible and a long moment of silence. No one tells the young people how to pray, they just do it by joining the community in prayer. The brothers explain that "the time of silence is to allow Jesus to speak within us,

then one day we shall discover that the depths of our being are inhabited by a Presence".

The aim is to allow the Spirit of God to pray in each person.

On 16th August 2005, Brother Roger died as he lived, praying with the community. He was stabbed to death by a mentally-disturbed woman during the evening prayer service attended by 2,500 people.

He was ninety years of age.

Eight years before his death, Brother Roger, a Protestant, appointed Brother Alois, a German Catholic, to be his successor. While everyone mourned the loss of Brother Roger, Brother Alois reminds us, "That even if Brother Roger was the heart of our lives, we are centred on Jesus Christ. He never pointed to himself, but to God, the living presence of God".

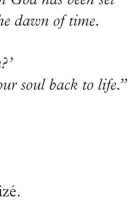

Today, small groups of brothers are present in Asia, Africa and South America. They strive to be a presence of love among the very poor, street children, prisoners, the dying and those who are wounded by broken relationships or by being abandoned.

"The desire for communion with God has been set within the human heart since the dawn of time. And so we say to Jesus, 'to whom shall we go but to you?' You have the words that bring our soul back to life."
Brother Roger

Pause to Reflect

Watch the Power Point presentation of Taizé.

Activities

1. Work in small groups. Watch the video of Taizé. (DVD ROM)
   a) Why do you think Taizé attracts so many young people?
   b) In what ways do you think the experience may help and challenge them?

2. Produce a 'Guide to Taizé'.
   • Background and origins;
   • what to expect;
   • where to go;
   • things to do;
   • benefits.
   Or use 'Movie Maker' to make a visual and audio guide.

Challenges for Us

Jesus knew what life would be like for us so he told the parable of the Sower. Let us study this parable, discover the meaning of it and find out how it might help us to prepare for mission.

1. a) **Read the Parable of the Sower,** Luke 8:4-15.

(i) Those that fell by the path.

(iii) Those that fell among thorns.

(ii) Those that fell on rocky places.

(iv) Those that fell on good ground.

   b) Give the meaning of each type of seed as described in the parable.
   c) In what ways is the parable relevant to the mission of the Church? How might it help us to prepare for mission?

Pressures versus Opportunities

We have studied the mission of the Church in a variety of situations and places. We have seen how God's Spirit is at work in people who are fully alive and carrying on the mission of Jesus.

Now we need to look specifically at young people in the Church today. Let us take time to identify some of the **pressures** and **opportunities** they face in trying to carry out the mission.

Pressures:

- peer pressure from friends;
- pressure to join gangs;
- academic pressure from parents and school;
- psychological pressure from the media: 'must have', 'I want it and I want it now';
- pressure to win: 'you're nothing unless you win';
- pressure to cope with stress;
- temptation to use alcohol or drugs.

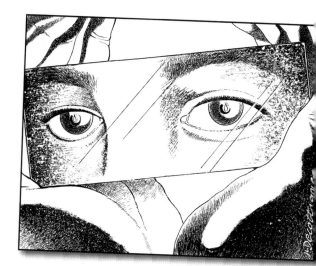

Opportunities:

- standing up for what you believe;
- rising above 'labels', for example, what you wear, where you come from;
- feeling part of the Church and finding friends to accompany you;
- finding faith in God, keeping it, living it, being it and doing it;
- discovering how and why we must forgive and what it means to take the first step.

Be a light to the World

In the Church, we listen to the Word of God and reflect on the meaning it has for our lives. In this way, we are drawn to a true understanding of ourselves, how to live in the light of God's word.

Jesus said, **"You are the light of the world. A city built on a hill-top cannot be hidden. No one lights a lamp to put it under a tub; they put it on a lamp-stand where it shines for everyone in the house. In the same way, your light must shine in the sight of people, so that, seeing your good works, they may give the praise to your Father in heaven."** (Mt. 5:14-16)

Pope John Paul II understood the pressures and challenges for young people:

"Young people, do not be afraid!
Do not be afraid of those deep desires you have for happiness, for truth, for beauty and for lasting love!

When I look at you, the young people, I feel great gratitude and hope. The future far into the next century lies in your hands. The future of peace lies in your hearts. To construct history, as you can and must, you must free history from the false paths it is pursuing ….

What I see arising in you is a new awareness of your responsibility and a fresh sensitivity to the needs of your fellow human beings. You are touched by the hunger for peace that so many share with you. You are troubled by so much injustice around you. You sense overwhelming danger in the gigantic stockpiles of arms and in the threats of nuclear war. You suffer when you see widespread hunger and malnutrition. You are concerned about the environment today and for the coming generations." Pope John Paul II's Message to mark the World Day of Peace, 1st January 1985.

How can we make sure that we can truly be a light to the world?

It will not happen if we rely only on our own resources. Just as our physical body needs food to sustain it, so our spiritual life needs the sacraments. It is in the sacraments that we meet God. "God comes to us and acts in our lives in a way that does not depend on what we feel or whether we experience strong emotions. He comes to us in the sacraments, silently and strongly. He comes into the very depth of our being. God is at work in the sacraments of the Church with certainty and sureness." Archbishop Vincent Nichols

Activities

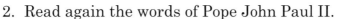

1. Work in groups.
    a) Dramatise the pressures on young people today.
    b) Show how their friends could help them cope.

2. Read again the words of Pope John Paul II.
    a) Pick out a part of the speech which most inspires you.
    b) Present it in a thoughtful eye-catching way.
    c) Explain underneath why you chose it.

3. Work in pairs. Imagine you are going to live in a country where ninety percent of the population are non-Christian. It is a secular state and the president is likely to welcome you as a missionary provided you can clearly explain
    • what your mission is;
    • the basis for it;
    • how it is likely to improve the quality of life for all the people.
    Think of all the aspects of the Church you have studied.
    Write to the president to provide the necessary information, or role-play the interview.

6. The Church in Britain

Know about the first arrival of the Gospel in Britain.
Reflect on the courage of the early Christians.

Arrival of the Gospel

After the resurrection, Jesus instructed his disciples to go out to the whole world to proclaim the **Good News** to all creation (Mk. 16:15). Jesus had risen from the dead. He had conquered death and opened the way to eternal life for everyone. His resurrection broke the power of sin and this meant that **good** will triumph.

The disciples set out on a **journey of faith**. Their story is one of excitement, adventure, bravery, selflessness, love, hardship, persecution and rejection. It is our story too for, through our Baptism, we are called to join this journey of faith.

Activity Work in groups. Make a collage of the 'Disciples' Journey of Faith'.
(Guidance in TB and on DVD ROM)

When did the Church come to Britain?

Christianity came to Britain soon after the death and resurrection of Jesus because both Palestine and Britain were part of the Roman Empire. So our story begins in Roman Britain that was part of a multi-cultural, multi-ethnic empire stretching from Turkey in the east, to the northern border with Scotland. Various religions, including Christianity, travelled with the Roman army to all corners of the known world.

Christianity: a threat

At this time, the Romans who were in positions of power saw Christianity as a threat. Why? It was because the Romans worshipped many gods and even considered their Emperor to be a god. To refuse to accept this was seen as treason. If people were even suspected of being Christian they were questioned.

> "I ask them if they are Christians. If they do not admit it, I repeat the question a second time, threatening them with capital punishment. If they persist, I sentence them to death …. For whatever kind of crime they have committed, they are so obstinate they should certainly be punished."
> (Pliny, a Roman Governor).

It became very dangerous to be a Christian. They had to live their faith in secret, but they still continued to spread the Good News wherever and whenever they could. Here is an example of one priest who was seeking refuge from the Romans.

St. Alban: The First British Martyr

The hour was late and Alban, a British soldier in the Roman army, was on the point of going to bed, when the faint creak of the door leading into the courtyard of his villa, followed by the sound of whispering, caught his attention. Curious to know who could be calling at that time of night, Alban walked quietly towards the door, where, to his surprise, he saw one of his slaves talking to an elderly man. On seeing his master, the slave stepped back in terror but the stranger moved quietly between the two men and faced Alban, who demanded to know what was going on. The man gave his name as Amphibalus and throwing himself on the mercy of Alban explained that he was a priest who had fled from the town because he would not worship the Emperor. He begged for shelter for the night.

Alban listened in astonishment. He had heard of the Christians but could not understand why they were so stubborn in their refusal to give worship to the Emperor. However, he decided to allow the man to stay for the night before deciding what to do with him. Over the next few days, Alban and Amphibalus spent many hours talking and Alban came to know about Jesus. Although it was very dangerous to give shelter to Christians, Alban found that he could not hand the Christian priest over to the governor to be tortured and killed.

Then, without warning, soldiers arrived at the villa. Alban hurriedly put on the priest's clothes and was promptly arrested and dragged before the governor. On discovering the deception, the governor was furious and demanded that Alban should immediately worship the Emperor or suffer death. Alban declared "I am called Alban and I worship and adore the true and living God who created all things". Alban refused to betray his

faith in Jesus and, after being tortured, was taken to a hill at Verulamium in Hertfordshire. His courage and faith were so strong that he impressed one of the executioners and he too begged to be allowed to die for Jesus. The two men were beheaded and their witness of faith led many others to become Christians.

A church was eventually built on the site and it became a shrine and a centre of pilgrimage. A monastery was founded there and the town of St. Albans grew up around it.

Activities

1. What do you think?
   a) Why didn't Alban hand the priest over to the governor?
   b) Why did Alban refuse to give in to the threats of the governor?
   c) What did his death show to those around him?
   d) What does it mean to you?

2. Work in groups.
   a) The priest and Alban talked late into the night. Here are some of the questions Alban may have asked. What answers do you think the priest gave him?
   • Who is Jesus?
   • Why did he come to earth?
   • What did he do for us?
   • What did he say to the apostles before going back to heaven?
   • What is the link between your work and the apostles?
   b) What other questions do you think Alban asked?
   c) Share your questions and answers with the class

Know about the first missionaries to Britain.
Reflect on the message they have for us today.

The First Missionaries

On 3rd February 313 AD, the Emperor Constantine declared that Christians would be allowed to practise their faith freely and without fear of persecution. He himself was baptised a Christian. However, within a hundred years, the Roman Empire was in decline. The last of the Roman legions left England in 410 AD, and the country was invaded and raided by Angles, Saxons and Jutes. These did not believe in Jesus; they were known as pagans. Christian communities only survived in parts of the west of England and Wales.

However, the history of the Church in Britain and Ireland spans many centuries. It will not be possible to cover all aspects of it in this book. Our aim is to highlight some of the most important people, for example St. Augustine, and invite you to do your own research on the others.

Important among these early missionaries were
- St. Patrick
- St. Columba
- St. Brigid
- St. David
- St. Aidan
- St. Hilda
- St. Bede.

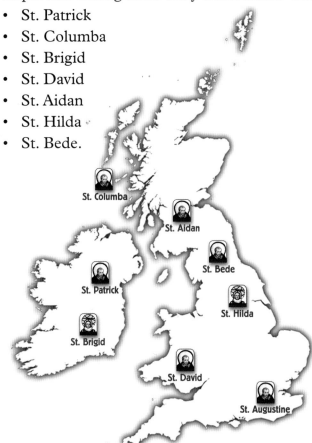

Activity

Work in small groups. Make a display of aspects of the early Church in Britain. Start by choosing one of the saints on the left.

Be sure to cover:
- where and when the person lived;
- what you think is most noteworthy about his/her life;
- why the person is still remembered.
- Does this person have a message for us today?

Each group makes a presentation of the saint they have researched.
(Information about the saints is on the DVD ROM)

St. Augustine and the Benedictine Monks

Despite the preaching of the Celtic missionaries, many in England followed non-Christian religions. In 597 AD, Pope Gregory decided to send missionaries to England. He chose Augustine who was a monk in St. Andrew's Monastery in Rome to lead the mission.

Augustine arrived on the Kent coast with forty monks. He sent a message to King Ethelbert telling him that they had come from Rome with *"good news of everlasting joy in heaven, and a kingdom that knows no end, with the true and living God"*.

The King told them to stay where they were until he decided what to do with them. Eventually, out of curiosity, he went to hear what the missionaries had to say. Fearful that they might use magic on him, he held the meeting in the open air. He was very impressed by what they had to say, but was cautious and did not convert immediately. However, within a few months the King became a Christian. He gave the monks a large building in Canterbury and allowed them to preach freely.

Before long, many people became Christians. St. Bede wrote about them: *"Then greater numbers began to come together to hear the Word and to forsake their heathen ways and join the Church. The King was known to be pleased at their faith and conversion, not that he would drive anyone to the Christian fold, for those who prepared him for baptism had taught him that one must choose to serve Jesus Christ, not be forced to it"*.

This mission was so successful that St. Augustine was soon able to send his monks to convert other countries in Europe to Christianity.

Activity

King Ethelbert made many wise decisions.
Find evidence for four of them in the above text.

Understand that there was a struggle between the Church and the State.
Reflect on the importance of making decisions about our Faith.

St. Thomas Becket – I am willing to die

One of the most well known martyrs of the early Church was called Thomas Becket who was born in London about fifty years after the Normans conquered Britain in 1066. By this time, the Church was well established. Monasteries were flourishing, and the Church had become increasingly powerful and rich.

Thomas Becket had worked for the Archbishop of Canterbury and was also a friend of the king, Henry II. In 1155, Thomas was appointed Chancellor – a very powerful position in the government. When Theobald, the Archbishop of Canterbury, died in 1163, Thomas Becket was made archbishop. This made him the most senior churchman in the country.

There was tension between the king and the Church over taxes, the legal system and the appointment of bishops. King Henry II thought that by having his friend, Thomas Becket, in the top position, he would be able to have more control over the Church. But Thomas Becket was faced with a choice: to follow the agenda of the king or to consider his duty to God and the Church first. He decided that God and the Church demanded his total loyalty, so he resigned as Chancellor.

This led to many arguments between Thomas Becket and King Henry II, and even to Thomas being exiled to France for six years. However, when he returned in 1170, he was still determined to act according to his conscience. He stood firm by what he believed to be the right things to do, that is, what he believed God wanted. Eventually, on 29th December 1170, the king was so angry after a row with Thomas, he shouted: "What cowards are round me that no one will free me of this low-born priest?"

Four of the king's knights thought this was an order for the archbishop to be killed, so they set off for Canterbury Cathedral. They found Thomas Becket in the church with a monk, Edward Grim, who afterwards wrote about what happened. This is how he described the death of Thomas Becket:

Full of anger; the knights called out, 'Where is Thomas Becket, traitor to the King?' At this, with outstretched arms, Thomas said: 'Here am I, a servant of God, not a traitor to the King'. Having said this, he turned to the right, under a pillar, by the altar of the Virgin Mary.

Then, they laid evil hands on him, dragging him so that they might kill him outside the church. But they could not pull him from the pillar. Then, seeing that he was about to die, he bowed his head and, joining his hands, he lifted them up and prayed to the Virgin Mary.

He had barely spoken when a wicked guard suddenly leapt on him, and wounded him on the head..... and by the same blow; he wounded the arm of him who tells this. He was given a second blow to the head, but still stood firm. At the third blow, he fell to his hands and knees, saying in a low voice: 'For the name of Jesus, I am ready to die.' Then, the third knight gave him a terrible wound as he lay there, so that the sword broke against the stone floor... The fourth knight stopped anyone interfering...

In 1173, the Pope declared that Thomas Becket was a saint, and the following year, King Henry II – who was truly sorry for what had happened – travelled to Canterbury Cathedral to visit the place where the archbishop died, to do penance and to pray at his grave.

Activity

Imagine you are a journalist writing an article on the murder of Thomas Becket:
- you interview the King and report on his side of the events;
- give your own opinion about why you think there was conflict between Thomas and the King.

Henry VIII and the break from Rome

Until about 1530, the Catholic religion was the common faith all over Europe and the British Isles. By the beginning of the 16th century, Europe was torn by wars of a political and religious nature. There was change everywhere. This affected the Church in Britain. The Pope in Rome was head of the Church in England as well as throughout the world. King Henry VIII was loyal to the Pope. He had no sympathy with the attacks on the Church by Martin Luther, who was the initiator of the Reformation which led to the development of the Protestant Church in Germany.

If you look at any British coin you will see, on the 'heads' side, the letters F.D. or Fid. Def. These stand for *Fidei Defensor* which means 'Defender of the Faith'. This title was given to Henry VIII by the Pope in 1521 for writing a book *'Defence of the Seven Sacraments'*, against Luther's idea that there were only two sacraments – Baptism and the Eucharist.

By the late 1520s, however, Henry's feelings were changing towards the Pope. In 1509, he had married Catherine of Aragon, a Spanish princess. They had one surviving child, a daughter, Mary. Henry was desperate for a son to succeed him but, following several unsuccessful pregnancies, Catherine seemed unable to provide him with one. So Henry decided, for dynastic reasons, to ask the Pope for an annulment of his marriage in order to marry Anne Boleyn with whom he had fallen in love.

For Catholics, a marriage can be declared null (that means not truly a marriage) only if there are good reasons, which prove that the marriage was invalid from its very beginnings. In the teaching of Jesus Christ, a valid marriage lasts for a lifetime. In King Henry's case, the decision to annul his marriage could only be made under the authority of the Pope. The Pope was not willing to declare Henry VIII's marriage null. As a result, relations between the Pope and Henry grew worse: Henry, ignoring the Church, divorced Catherine and married Anne; they had a daughter, Elizabeth.

1. Work in pairs. Imagine you are Marriage Counsellors for the Church. What advice might you give to Henry VIII and Catherine of Aragon in 1520?
Consider:
   - was it necessary to get a divorce;
   - offer alternatives;
   - give the teaching of Jesus on divorce;
   - offer advice and encouragement on the best way forward for them and for the country.

2. a) Watch the Power Point presentation 'Formation of Conscience'.
   b) In your opinion did King Henry VIII act on an informed conscience when he divorced Catherine of Aragon? Give reasons for your answer.

St. Thomas More

Thomas More, a brilliant lawyer, was the Lord Chancellor of England. King Henry VIII liked him and used to visit his home in Chelsea. However, Thomas knew that the King's marriage to Catherine of Aragon was valid and he could not agree with his decision to divorce her in order to marry Anne Boleyn. Because of this, he resigned his office as Chancellor and so had to live with his family in relative poverty in comparison with his earlier lifestyle.

The dispute over Henry's marriage led to the breaking of England's links with the universal Catholic Church. From 1533, Henry VIII began the break away from the Church by a series of Acts of Parliament. **The Act of Supremacy declared Henry VIII to be the Supreme Head of the Church in England.**

On 14th April 1534, Thomas More was summoned to take the Oath of Supremacy but refused and was sent to the Tower of London on a charge of high treason against the Crown. He was imprisoned for over a year, and during this time he could not be persuaded or bribed to change his mind. He was frequently ill. Even his writing materials were taken away, but he managed to write letters with a bit of charcoal.

His favourite daughter, Meg, was allowed to visit him. Her efforts to try to persuade him to take the Oath were in vain.

After a trial, at which false evidence was presented against him, he was condemned to death for high treason.

Pause to Reflect

Listen to the audio recording of the Trial. (DVD ROM)

Execution of St. Thomas More

Thomas remained serene and calm, his mind was free and he felt close to God. Thomas was beheaded on Tower Hill in London on 6th July 1535. At the place of execution he said to the crowds:

"I die the King's Good Servant, but God's first."

He was canonised in 1935 and he was declared Patron Saint of politicians and statesmen by Pope John Paul II in 2000.

Activities

1. Thomas More's daughter, Meg, tried several times to persuade him to take the Oath of Supremacy. Was she right? Give reasons to support your answer showing that you have considered more than one point of view.

2. Imagine you are Thomas More. Write a final letter to your wife, Lady Alice More, explaining why you are unable to take the Oath of Supremacy. Try to keep your letter to two or three paragraphs and write in the present tense. Think about:
   • your loyalty to your family;
   • implications of your choice for others;
   • the reasons why you are standing firm;
   • the reasons why others are unable to agree with you (e.g. family, Henry VIII).

3. From 'Friend to Foe'! What made Henry VIII choose Thomas as a friend and then later have him put to death?

The Reformation

King Henry VIII eventually had a son, Edward, by his third wife, Jane Seymour. Henry still considered himself a Catholic. Although he had become Supreme Head of the Church in England, the Church under him still retained Catholic services.

King Henry VIII died in 1547 and his son became Edward VI. He was only nine years old when he became king and he was a Protestant. He supported the Archbishop of Canterbury, Thomas Cranmer, in bringing in Protestant reforms of the Church in England and Wales.

In 1549, Parliament changed the liturgy. They issued and made compulsory the Book of Common Prayer, which replaced the Catholic Missal. The English translation of the Bible was also used in church; up to this time it had been in Latin. Protestants felt it was wrong to have pictures and statues. They wanted plain churches and services in English so that they could be understood. They did not want to accept the teaching authority of the Pope in Rome regarding the liturgy and the sacraments.

As the division between Catholics loyal to Rome and Protestants grew, the two groups began to interpret and practise their faith in different ways.

Return to the Catholic Church or be punished

When Edward died in July 1553, Henry VIII's daughter by Catherine of Aragon, Mary, succeeded to the throne. Mary was a devout Catholic. Catholic bishops were reinstated and the doctrines of the Catholic Church were taught once more. Protestants who did not wish to live under Catholic rule were free to leave the country.

Mary I was determined to re-establish the Catholic Church in England, but many objected to it. As a consequence, around three hundred Protestant men and women were burned at the stake, and many more were imprisoned for their faith. Mary reigned for five turbulent years. People had now been forced to take sides: either Catholic or Protestant.

Mary died in 1558, and her half-sister, Elizabeth I, became queen. She formulated an Anglican Settlement and established the legal basis of the Church of England. She took the title of 'Supreme Governor of the Realm in Matters Spiritual and Temporal'. The thirty-nine Articles defining Anglican belief were published.

Kings & Queens	Henry VIII 1509-1547 (Catholic)	Edward VI 1547-1553 (Protestant)	Mary I 1553-1558 (Catholic)	Elizabeth I 1558-1603 (Protestant)
Head of Church	King replaced Pope as Head of the Church	King was Head of the Church	Pope became Head of Church again	Queen became 'Governor' of the Church-hoping to please Catholics and Protestants
Church Services	Little change. Still in Latin.	Services in English	Services in Latin	Services in English
Prayers	'Our Father' in English, but most others stayed in Latin	New Prayer Book with prayers in English	New Prayer book banned	New Prayer Book with prayers in English
Bible	In English	In English	In English	In English
Priests	Not allowed to marry	Priests could marry	Priests and wives had to part	Priests could marry again

Conform to the Church of England or be punished

In the reign of Queen Elizabeth I, two Acts of Parliament in 1559 called the 'Act of Supremacy' and the 'Act of Uniformity', gave the monarch full authority over the Church of England and required all people to conform to it.

In 1570, the Pope excommunicated Elizabeth. The rift between Rome and England was going to be long lasting and severe.

Punishments for those refusing to give up their Catholic Faith
(1) If a person spoke against the new religion they would be fined and the fine was increased for a second offence.
(2) Their goods and possessions would all be confiscated if they persisted in criticising the Church of England.
(3) Everyone was expected to attend the Sunday service in his or her parish church. If they didn't, they would be fined a shilling, which was a day's wages for a skilled worker.
(4) In 1563, Parliament introduced the death penalty for anyone convicted a second time of refusing to accept that the Queen was the Supreme Governor of the Church in England.

About eighty per cent of the population conformed to the Church of England to avoid the fines or other punishments. Those who remained loyal to the Catholic Church included about five hundred priests. They were not allowed to celebrate Mass or preach in England, but some were prepared to risk their lives rather than leave the people without the sacraments. They knew that if they were caught they would be tortured and executed. Those who wished to study for the priesthood had to go to the English College at Douai, northern France which was a new seminary founded in 1568 or to the English College in Rome which opened in 1579.

Over three hundred Catholics, one hundred of whom were priests, were executed during the reign of Elizabeth. Of those, forty have been canonised martyrs.

Activity

a) **Choose one of the Forty Martyrs.**
b) **Make a fact file of his/her life.**
c) **Use your information for a class display.**

Priests' Hiding Holes

Despite the dangers, many Catholic families took great risks to hide Catholic priests and built secret places in their homes where priests could hide to escape detection. These were known as 'priest holes'. Fr. William Weston hid in one when what he called the 'heretics' burst into the house where he had been celebrating Mass.

Fr. William Weston wrote:

From my cave-like hide, I could follow their movements by the noise and uproar they raised. Step by step, they drew closer, and when they entered my room, the sight of my books was an added incentive to their search. In that room there was also a secret passage to which they demanded the key, and as they opened the door onto it, they were standing immediately above my head. I could hear practically every word they said. 'Here, look!' they called out. 'A chalice! And a missal!' Then they demanded a hammer and other tools to break through the wall and panelling. They were certain now that I could not be far away ...

Fr. John Gerard SJ described how he was once cornered in a house and had to remain literally holed up in a wall for four days without food or water while a team tore up the floorboards and stripped the plaster off the wall around him. Despite their efforts, they did not find him.

Pause to Reflect

Watch the Power Point presentation on the Priests' Hiding Holes.
- Why do you think the priests risked their lives to celebrate the Mass?
- The families who sheltered the priests also risked their lives. Why do you think they did this?

St. Edmund Campion

Edmund Campion was one of the most famous of the martyrs. He was born in 1540 and brought up an Anglican. He showed signs of a brilliant intellect and won a scholarship to Oxford University when he was only fifteen years old. While at Oxford he began to have doubts about the Church of England. He left the university and after a period of reflection in Ireland he went to Douai in Northern France and then to Rome where he eventually became a Jesuit priest.

In 1580, he was sent back to England to support and guide the Catholics who were very confused about laws forbidding them to attend Mass. Even though he wore clothes to disguise his priesthood, people were flocking to him for the Mass and to hear him preach.

From his hideout, Edmund Campion wrote:

"In the house where I am, all the talk is of death, fleeing, prison or the ruin of friends yet they keep going with courage … Nor will this (Catholic) Church fail … Rumours of approaching danger force me to end this letter here."

Secretly, he published a paper outlining the ten reasons on which the Catholic Church based its authority. Six weeks later, he was betrayed and captured.

On 1st December 1581, he was dragged behind a horse to Tyburn Hill, close to Marble Arch in London and there hanged, drawn and quartered.

Activity
Imagine you are a priest hiding in a priest-hole while the priest hunters break down the panelling.
   a) What thoughts are going through your mind?
   b) What are the implications for your host family?
   c) Attendance at Mass is punishable by death. What is so special about the Mass that you are willing to risk your life?

St. Margaret Clitherow

Margaret Clitherow was born in 1556 in York. Her family were Protestants. When she was fifteen years old, she married a butcher, John Clitherow. She was so inspired by the Catholics suffering for their faith that three years later, she became a Catholic and spent the next twelve years of her life sheltering and providing for the missionary priests.

In 1584, Margaret's eldest son Henry, aged twelve, went to the seminary in Douai. Soon his absence was noted and Margaret's husband was questioned and their house was searched. The first time, nothing was found, but the authorities returned again and found priests' hiding holes, vestments and hosts.

Margaret was arrested and accused of harbouring priests. She refused to enter a plea because she wanted to spare her children from being forced to give evidence against her. Finally, the judge passed sentence that she should be crushed to death. On 25th March 1586, she was taken to the place of execution. She was placed on a sharp stone with a board placed over her and huge stones were placed on the board. Fifteen minutes later she was dead. Her last words were: "Jesus, Jesus, Jesus, have mercy on me".

Activities

1. Margaret Clitherow was one of the very courageous women who offered shelter to fugitive priests, hiding them in a special room where she and other secret Catholics could attend Mass.
   a) Listen to the recording of an imaginary letter written by her to you. (DVD ROM)
   b) Now study the contents of the letter and write a reply. Take time to reflect on what you want to say and try to comment on each paragraph.

2. Faced with imprisonment, torture and death, Catholics could have simply said: "It would be better to swear allegiance to the king or queen rather than suffer and be killed." Why didn't they? Give reasons for your answer showing that you have considered more than one point of view. Think about:
   - conscience;
   - public witness;
   - faith;
   - service.

3. Reflect on the courage and conviction shown by the martyrs. What do we owe them? Discuss.

The Emancipation

It was almost two hundred years before Catholics in Britain were able to practise their Faith freely again, without fear of persecution. By the end of the 18th century, there were very few of them left; they had very little influence in State affairs or politics and were no longer seen as a threat.

The Relief Acts of 1778 and 1791 and the 1829 Emancipation Act, allowed Catholics almost total freedom.

Benefits to Catholics from the passing of the Emancipation Act

- It was no longer illegal to be a Catholic.
  They didn't need to fear arrest or punishment.

- Catholics were allowed to build churches and worship in them but many chose to build schools first.

- They were allowed to vote.

- They were allowed to stand as members of Parliament.
  Five Catholic MPs were elected in the General Election of 1830.

- The Roman Catholic Church could run its own affairs without interference from the State.

John Henry Newman (1801-1890)

John Henry Newman was an Anglican priest and a theologian at Oxford University. He made a very detailed study of the development of Christian doctrine with the intention of showing that the Anglican Church was the true Church. However, through this study, he was led to believe that the Catholic Church was the authentic one and could trace its origin back to the time of the apostles. As a result, in 1845 he became a Catholic. Later, he became a cardinal and was regarded as a very distinguished person in the Church.

He described what it was like for Catholics in the early nineteenth century:

No longer the Catholic Church in the country; nay, no longer, I may say, a Catholic community, but a few adherents of the Old Religion, moving silently and sorrowfully about, as memorials of what had been.

There, perhaps, an elderly person, seen walking in the streets, grave and solitary, and strange though noble in bearing, and said to be of goodly family, and a 'Roman Catholic'. An old-fashioned house of gloomy appearance closed in with high walls, with an iron gate, and yews, and the report attaching to it that 'Roman Catholics' lived there; but who they were, and what they did, or what was meant by calling them Roman Catholics, no one could tell – though it had an unpleasant sound, and told of form and superstition.

Pause to Reflect

- Slowly re-read the description of what it was like for Catholics in the 1840s.
- Now think about the freedom and opportunities you have today.
- Reflect on how you use your freedom.
- Take time to thank God for all He makes available to you.

Revival of the Catholic Church

The number of Catholics began to grow and, in 1850, England and Wales could once again be divided into dioceses with a bishop in each one.

Nicholas Wiseman was the first Archbishop of Westminster to be appointed. He made it clear that the Catholic Church would not be a threat to government or politics, but that it would condemn the appalling conditions that many people lived in:

The labyrinth of lanes and courts, and alleys and slums, nests of ignorance, vice, depravity, and crime, as well as of squalor, wretchedness and disease; whose atmosphere is typhus, whose ventilation is cholera; in which swarms a huge and countless population, in great measure, nominally at least, Catholic; haunts of filth, which no sewage committee can reach, dark corners, which no lighting boards can brighten …

Activity

In Britain, we are now able to practise our faith, free from fear of persecution. Imagine that a regime opposed to Christianity took over and you were not allowed to practise.
a) What would change for you and your family?
b) What difference would it make to your life?

Glossary

Abortion – an operation or other intervention to end the pregnancy by removing the foetus (unborn baby) from the womb

Accordance – agreement; harmony

Adherents – people who follow certain traditions or practices

Annulment – a declaration stating that the marriage was invalid from the very beginning

Animated – alive

Archangel – a chief messenger of God

Atheist – a person who does not believe in the existence of God

Beatified – declared 'Blessed' by the Catholic Church; to state officially that this person led a holy life as the first step towards canonisation

Brigand – a member of a band of robbers

Calvary – a hill outside the walls of Jerusalem where criminals were executed

Cardinal – a priest who has been an archbishop and is now next in rank to the pope and acts as an adviser to him

Cannibalism – the eating of human flesh

Chametz – any food that is made of grain and water that has been allowed to rise, e.g. bread, cake, biscuits

Conception – formation in the womb

Consecration – to make holy; dedicate to the service of God

Defilement – pollution

Descendants – ancestors

Dignity – deserving of respect

Diocese – a certain area in a country for which a bishop is responsible

Divinity – being God

Dominion – authority to rule

Emancipation – being freed from rules, freed to carry on without restrictions or fear

Eucharist – it actually means 'thanksgiving'; also it is sometimes used for the Mass or for the body and blood of Jesus

Euthanasia – to bring about the death of someone with an incurable or a painful disease

Fatal mistake – a mistake that ends in death

Firmament – the sky with its clouds and stars

High priest – the senior Jewish leader

Holy Week – the very special week for Christians leading up to Easter Sunday

House of Judah – Southern Kingdom

House of Israel – Northern Kingdom

Immaculate – free from stain; spotless

Incarcerated – in prison

Infidelity – unfaithfulness; letting someone down

Invalid – not valid, not legally binding

Last Supper – the meal associated with the

Passover, which Jesus celebrated with his disciples in the upper room the night before he died

Liturgy – worshipping God in public

Liturgy of the Word – readings from the Old and New Testament

Manifestation – a sign

Manna – bread; originally the food eaten by Moses and his followers in the desert of Sinai

Messiah – the Saviour sent by God to save His people from their sins; a Hebrew word meaning 'anointed One'; in Greek 'the Christ'

Miraculous – an extraordinary event attributed to supernatural power

Monastery – a building with grounds in which a group of people (monks) observe religious vows and live together

Offertory – that part of the Mass in which the unconsecrated bread and wine are offered to God shortly before the consecration

Omniscience – God's power to know everything.

Paschal candle – Easter candle

Paschal Mystery – the mystery of the passion, death and resurrection of Jesus

Penitential Rite – it is a form of words we use when we ask for forgiveness and healing for any sin that separates us from each other and from God, and in which we receive God's forgiveness

Pesach – Passover

Psychology – the study of the mind and how it works

Rabbi – a Jewish scholar qualified to teach or interpret Jewish law

Roman governor – the senior Roman in an occupied territory; the Emperor's representative

Sabbath – the day of rest, Saturday for Jews and Sunday for Christians

Sacrifice – by itself, it means the offering of something to God, for example Old Testament sacrifice. As applied to the Eucharist, it is the highest form of adoration which the priest makes present again Jesus Christ's offering of himself to the Father. The priest also offers himself and the people with Christ's offering of self to God the Father.

Salvation – being saved; being united with God

Sanhedrin – the Jews' ruling council

Secular humanism – a world view that stresses human values without reference to religion or spirituality

Sustain – support

Theology – by itself, the study or science of God; for us it is the study of the Christian faith and of God's plan of love for human beings, the world and the whole universe

Treason – opposing and threatening the government or the leader of the State (emperor, king, etc.)

Upper room – the room where Jesus and his disciples celebrated the Last Supper and where he appeared to them after his resurrection

Wrath – anger

Zealots – a member of a group of Jewish rebels

Acknowledgements

Considerable thanks are due to those teachers who commented on various drafts of the Student's Book, 'The Truth', as well as to the Editorial Team.

Permission credits

Cover photo: stained glass window © CWS Design, 9 Ferguson Drive, Lisburn BT28 2EX; forest © Anthia Cumming Dreamstime.com; Pen and Pad – used throughout © Kjpargeter Dreamstime.com; Wise Owl – used throughout © Joingate Dreamstime.com; Peace Dove – used throughout © Ginesvaler Dreamstime.com; pages 4, 5, 6,9, 16, 17,20, 22, 47, 57, 58, 62, 63, 70, 76 photos © Sr. Marcellina Cooney CP; pages 6, 39, 41, 45, 61, 67, 90, 91 © Sr. Mary Stephen CRSS and McCrimmon Publishing Co. Ltd; page 8 Mille Images Symboliques, © Patrick Royer, Les Presses d'Ile de France; pages 10, 65, 68 by Elizabeth Wang, © Radiant Light; pages 10, 11, 86 © CWS Design; pages 12, 25, 27, 40 stained glass windows from St. Luke's Catholic Church, Dunmury, Belfast BT17 Diocese of Down & Connor, photos used with permission from Rev Darach Mac Giolla Catháin; pages 14, 15 stained glass windows from Our Lady Queen of Peace Catholic Church, Kilwee, Belfast BT17, used with permission from Very Rev Colm McBride PP; Earth Lightbulb, page 17 © Stephan Koscheck Dreamstime.com; page 18 and 106 Jesuits Yearbooks 2007, 2010 © permission from Jose M. de Vera SJ; page 19 © Ryan's Well Foundation. Page 21 © Dorothy M. Speiser; page 22 © Sisters of Notre Dame de Namur; p. 32 © Specialist Stock; pages 33 and 34 © Corbis; 3D Heart, page 43 © Eraxion Dreamstime.com; page 45 Mille Images d'Église by Jean-François Kieffer; pages 46, 74, 75, 77, 78, 80, 81, 82, 83 © ITV Global Entertainment; page 49 Mille Image d' Évangile by Jean- François Kieffer; page 53 © Sieger Köder, Abendmahl; pages 55 and 106 Mille Dimanches et Fêtes by Jean-Yves Decottignies; page 84 stained glass window from Our Lady of Dolours Catholic Church, Barnet NW4 used with permission from Rev Dominic Byrne PP; Globe, page 93 © Zash Dreamstime.com; pages 95, 96 photos used with permission of SVP; pages 97 and 98 photos used with permission of Mariana Clavero, Centro de Estudios Padre Hurtado, Chile; heart key, page 101 © Benjamin Gelman Dreamstime.com; key – page 101 © Victoria Suhanova Dreamstime.com; pages 102, 103 and 104 photos by Sabine Leutenegger © Ateliers et Presses de Taizé, 71250 Taizé, France; page 106 photo stained glass window in St. Colmcille Catholic Church, Kingsisland, Coalisland, Co. Tyrone photo by Susan Lawless and used with permission of Rev B. Fee PP; pages 110, 114,122, 124 photos by Fabio Ravà © Venerable English College, Rome; Great Britain Map, page 111 © Jiri Moucka Dreamstime.com; pages 112, 115 and 118 © copyright Topham PicturePoint; page 113 used with permission of Paul Mullineaux, Lancaster Priory; page 116 photo by Sr. Marcellina Cooney CP of stained glass window in St. Joseph's Convent Chapel, Hendon NW4 used with permission of Sr. Anthony O'Rourke, Poor Handmaids of Jesus Christ; page 121 stained glass window in Stoneyhurst College reproduced with permission of the Society of Jesus; page 123 stained glass window in St. George's Catholic Church, Wembley, used with permission of Rev Tony Seeldrayers PP.

Text Permission Credits

Page 12 'A Life That Matters' by kind permission of author, Clarissa Pinkola Estés, and publisher, © copyright 2009, all rights reserved, permissions projectscreener:aol.com; page 32 'Long hours and late pay' pages 98-99 Slavery © Danny Smith, Kingsway Publications; page 55 'Truth' was originally published in 'Conkers' (OUP and is reproduced with permission of Barrie Wade).

Every effort has been made to contact copyright holders of material used in this publication. Any omissions will be rectified in subsequent printings if notice is given to the Teachers' Enterprise in Religious Education Co. Ltd, 40 Duncan Terrace, London N1 8AL.